About the autho[r]

The same expert authors who produce *Practical [*
compiled At Court: Ancillary Relief Authorities an[
Blair QC; Peter Clark, Partner at Dawson Cornw[
Withers; and Richard Todd, Barrister.

Practical Matrimonial Precedents

Practical Matrimonial Precedents was first published in 1988. Its two loose-leaf volumes are updated twice a year to provide a comprehensive and up-to-the-minute guide to precedents and procedures in family proceedings.

Contents

A   Authorities and Forms

B   Evidence

C   Orders

A   Authorities and Forms

A(a) Matrimonial Causes Act 1973

Sections 22 to 25D, 28 to 33A and 37 of the Matrimonial Causes Act 1973

---

22 Maintenance pending suit   A1

On a petition for divorce, nullity of marriage or judicial separation, the court may make an order for maintenance pending suit, that is to say, an order requiring either party to the marriage to make to the other such periodical payments for his or her maintenance and for such term, being a term beginning not earlier than the date of the presentation of the petition and ending with the date of the determination of the suit, as the court thinks reasonable.

23 Financial provision orders in connection with divorce proceedings, etc.   A2

(1) On granting a decree of divorce, a decree of nullity of marriage or a decree of judicial separation or at any time thereafter (whether, in the case of a decree of divorce or of nullity of marriage, before or after the decree is made absolute), the court may make any one or more of the following orders, that is to say—

(a) an order that either party to the marriage shall make to the other such periodical payments, for such term, as may be specified in the order;

(b) an order that either party to the marriage shall secure to the other to the satisfaction of the court such periodical payments, for such term, as may be so specified;

(c) an order that either party to the marriage shall pay to the other such lump sum or sums as may be so specified;

(d) an order that a party to the marriage shall make to such person as may be specified in the order for the benefit of a child of the family, or to such a child, such periodical payments, for such term, as may be so specified;

(e) an order that a party to the marriage shall secure to such person as may be so specified for the benefit of such a child, or to such a child, to the satisfaction of the court, such periodical payments, for such term, as may be so specified;

1

    (f)   an order that a party to the marriage shall pay to such person as may be so specified for the benefit of such a child, or to such a child, such lump sum as may be so specified;

subject, however, in the case of an order under paragraph (d), (e) or (f) above, to the restrictions imposed by section 29(1) and (3) below on the making of financial provision orders in favour of children who have attained the age of eighteen.

    (2) The court may also, subject to those restrictions, make any one or more of the orders mentioned in subsection (1)(d), (e) and (f) above—

    (a)   in any proceedings for divorce, nullity of marriage or judicial separation, before granting a decree; and

    (b)   where any such proceedings are dismissed after the beginning of the trial, either forthwith or within a reasonable period after the dismissal.

    (3) Without prejudice to the generality of subsection (1)(c) or (f) above—

    (a)   an order under this section that a party to a marriage shall pay a lump sum to the other party may be made for the purpose of enabling that other party to meet any liabilities or expenses reasonably incurred by him or her in maintaining himself or herself or any child of the family before making an application for an order under this section in his or her favour;

    (b)   an order under this section for the payment of a lump sum to or for the benefit of a child of the family may be made for the purpose of enabling any liabilities or expenses reasonably incurred by or for the benefit of that child before the making of an application for an order under this section in his favour to be met; and

    (c)   an order under this section for the payment of a lump sum may provide for the payment of that sum by instalments of such amount as may be specified in the order and may require the payment of the instalments to be secured to the satisfaction of the court.

    (4) The power of the court under subsection (1) or (2)(a) above to make an order in favour of a child of the family shall be exercisable from time to time; and where the court makes an order in favour of a child under subsection (2)(b) above, it may from time to time, subject to the restrictions mentioned in subsection (1) above, make a further order in his favour of any of the kinds mentioned in subsection (1)(d), (e) or (f) above.

    (5) Without prejudice to the power to give a direction under section 30 below for the settlement of an instrument by conveyancing counsel, where an order is made under subsection (1)(a), (b) or (c) above on or after granting a decree of divorce or nullity of marriage, neither the order nor any settlement made in pursuance of the order shall take effect unless the decree has been made absolute.

(6) Where the court—

(a) makes an order under this section for the payment of a lump of sum; and

(b) directs—

(i) that payment of that sum or any part of it shall be deferred; or

(ii) that that sum or any part of it shall be paid by instalments,

the court may order that the amount deferred or the instalments shall carry interest at such rate as may be specified by the order from such date, not earlier than the date of the order, as may be so specified, until the date when payment of it is due.

24 Property adjustment orders in connection with divorce proceedings, etc.   A3

(1) On granting a decree of divorce, a decree of nullity of marriage or a decree of judicial separation or at any time thereafter (whether, in the case of a decree of divorce or of nullity of marriage, before or after the decree is made absolute), the court may make any one or more of the following orders, that is to say—

(a) an order that a party to the marriage shall transfer to the other party, to any child of the family or to such person as may be specified in the order for the benefit of such a child such property as may be so specified, being property to which the first-mentioned party is entitled, either in possession or reversion;

(b) an order that a settlement of such property as may be so specified, being property to which a party to the marriage is so entitled, be made to the satisfaction of the court for the benefit of the other party to the marriage and of the children of the family or either or any of them;

(c) an order varying for the benefit of the parties to the marriage and of the children of the family or either or any of them any ante-nuptial or post-nuptial settlement (including such a settlement made by will or codicil) made on the parties to the marriage;

(d) an order extinguishing or reducing the interest of either of the parties to the marriage under any such settlement;

subject, however, in the case of an order under paragraph (a) above, to the restrictions imposed by section 29(1) and (3) below on the making of orders for a transfer of property in favour of children who have attained the age of eighteen.

(2) The court may make an order under subsection (1)(c) above notwithstanding that there are no children of the family.

(3) Without prejudice to the power to give a direction under section 30 below for the settlement of an instrument by conveyancing counsel, where an order is made under this section on or after granting a decree of divorce or nullity of marriage, neither the order nor any settlement made in pursuance of the order shall take effect unless the decree has been made absolute.

24A Orders for sale of property   A4

(1) Where the court makes under section 23 or 24 of this Act a secured periodical payments order, an order for the payment of a lump sum or a property adjustment order, then, on making that order or at any time thereafter, the court may make a further order for the sale of such property as may be specified in the order, being property in which or in the proceeds of sale of which either or both of the parties to the marriage has or have a beneficial interest, either in possession or reversion.

(2) Any order made under subsection (1) above may contain such consequential or supplementary provisions as the court thinks fit and, without prejudice to the generality of the foregoing provision, may include—

(a) provision requiring the making of a payment out of the proceeds of sale of the property to which the order relates, and

(b) provision requiring any such property to be offered for sale to a person, or class of persons, specified in the order.

(3) Where an order is made under subsection (1) above on or after the grant of a decree of divorce or nullity of marriage, the order shall not take effect unless the decree has been made absolute.

(4) Where an order is made under subsection (1) above, the court may direct that the order, or such provision thereof as the court may specify, shall not take effect until the occurrence of an event specified by the court or the expiration of a period so specified.

(5) Where an order under subsection (1) above contains a provision requiring the proceeds of sale of the property to which the order relates to be used to secure periodical payments to a party to the marriage, the order shall cease to have effect on the death or re-marriage of that person.

(6) Where a party to a marriage has a beneficial interest in any property, or in the proceeds of sale thereof, and some other person who is not a party to the marriage also has a beneficial interest in that property or in the proceeds of sale thereof, then, before deciding whether to make an order under this section in relation to that property, it shall be the duty of the court to give that other person an opportunity to make representations with respect to the order, and any

representations made by that other person shall be included among the circumstances to which the court is required to have regard under section 25(1) below.

25 Matters to which court is to have regard in deciding how to exercise its powers under ss. 23, 24 and 24A   A5

(1) It shall be the duty of the court in deciding whether to exercise its powers under section 23, 24 or 24A above and, if so, in what manner, to have regard to all the circumstances of the case, first consideration being given to the welfare while a minor of any child of the family who has not attained the age of eighteen.

(2) As regards the exercise of the powers of the court under section 23(1)(a), (b) or (c), 24 or 24A above in relation to a party to the marriage, the court shall in particular have regard to the following matters—

(a) the income, earning capacity, property and other financial resources which each of the parties to the marriage has or is likely to have in the foreseeable future, including in the case of earning capacity any increase in that capacity which it would in the opinion of the court be reasonable to expect a party to the marriage to take steps to acquire;

(b) the financial needs, obligations and responsibilities which each of the parties to the marriage has or is likely to have in the foreseeable future;

(c) the standard of living enjoyed by the family before the breakdown of the marriage;

(d) the age of each party to the marriage and the duration of the marriage;

(e) any physical or mental disability of either of the parties to the marriage;

(f) the contributions which each of the parties has made or is likely in the foreseeable future to make to the welfare of the family, including any contribution by looking after the home or caring for the family;

(g) the conduct of each of the parties, if that conduct is such that it would in the opinion of the court be inequitable to disregard it;

(h) in the case of proceedings for divorce or nullity of marriage, the value to each of the parties to the marriage of any benefit (for example, a pension) which, by reason of the dissolution or annulment of the marriage, that party will lose the chance of acquiring.

(3) As regards the exercise of the powers of the court under section 23(1)(d), (e) or (f), (2) or (4), 24 or 24A above in relation to a child of the family, the court shall in particular have regard to the following matters—

(a) the financial needs of the child;

(b) the income, earning capacity (if any), property and other financial resources of the child;

   (c) any physical or mental disability of the child;

   (d) the manner in which he was being and in which the parties to the marriage expected him to be educated or trained;

   (e) the considerations mentioned in relation to the parties to the marriage in paragraphs (a), (b), (c) and (e) of subsection (2) above.

(4) As regards the exercise of the powers of the court under section 23(1)(d), (e) or (f), (2) or (4), 24 or 24A above against a party to a marriage in favour of a child of the family who is not the child of that party, the court shall also have regard—

   (a) to whether that party assumed any responsibility for the child's maintenance, and, if so, to the extent to which, and the basis upon which, that party assumed such responsibility and to the length of time for which that party discharged such responsibility;

   (b) to whether in assuming and discharging such responsibility that party did so knowing that the child was not his or her own;

   (c) to the liability of any other person to maintain the child.

25A Exercise of court's powers in favour of party to marriage on decree of divorce or nullity of marriage   A6

(1) Where on or after the grant of a decree of divorce or nullity of marriage the court decides to exercise its powers under section 23(1)(a), (b) or (c), 24 or 24A above in favour of a party to the marriage, it shall be the duty of the court to consider whether it would be appropriate so to exercise those powers that the financial obligations of each party towards the other will be terminated as soon after the grant of the decree as the court considers just and reasonable.

(2) Where the court decides in such a case to make a periodical payments or secured periodical payments order in favour of a party to the marriage, the court shall in particular consider whether it would be appropriate to require those payments to be made or secured only for such term as would in the opinion of the court be sufficient to enable the party in whose favour the order is made to adjust without undue hardship to the termination of his or her financial dependence on the other party.

(3) Where on or after the grant of a decree of divorce or nullity of marriage an application is made by a party to the marriage for a periodical payments or secured periodical payments order in his or her favour, then, if the court considers that no continuing obligation should be imposed on either party to make or secure periodical payments in favour of the other, the court may dismiss the application with a direction that the applicant shall not be entitled to make any

further application in relation to that marriage for an order under section 23(1)(a) or (b) above.

Pension sharing: a number of amendments to the Matrimonial Causes Act 1973 come into force on December 1, 2000 (and a number are already in force for the purpose of permitting enabling regulations to be made). The text of the Act as printed here reflects the law as it is applicable to the powers of the court before December 1, 2000.

25B Pensions   A7

(1) The matters to which the court is to have regard under section 25(2) above include—

(a) in the case of paragraph (a), any benefits under a pension scheme which a party to the marriage has or is likely to have, and

(b) in the case of paragraph (h), any benefits under a pension scheme which, by reason of the dissolution or annulment of the marriage, a party to the marriage will lose the chance of acquiring, and, accordingly, in relation to benefits under a pension scheme, section 25(2)(a) above shall have effect as if "in the foreseeable future" were omitted.

(2) In any proceedings for a financial provision order under section 23 above in a case where a party to the marriage has, or is likely to have, any benefit under a pension scheme, the court shall, in addition to considering any other matter which it is required to consider apart from this subsection, consider—

(a) whether, having regard to any matter to which it is required to have regard in the proceedings by virtue of subsection (1) above, such an order (whether deferred or not) should be made, and

(b) where the court determines to make such an order, how the terms of the order should be affected, having regard to any such matter.

(3) The following provisions apply where, having regard to any benefits under a pension scheme, the court determines to make an order under section 23 above.

(4) To the extent to which the order is made having regard to any benefits under a pension scheme, the order may require the trustees or managers of the pension scheme in question, if at any time any payment in respect of any benefits under the scheme becomes due to the party with pension rights, to make a payment for the benefit of the other party.

(5) The amount of any payment which, by virtue of subsection (4) above, the trustees or managers are required to make under the order at any time shall not exceed the amount of the payment which is due at that time to the party with pension rights.

(6) Any such payment by the trustees or managers—

(a) shall discharge so much of the trustees' or managers' liability to the party with pension rights as corresponds to the amount of the payment, and

(b) shall be treated for all purposes as a payment made by the party with pension rights in or towards the discharge of his liability under the order.

(7) Where the party with pension rights may require any benefits which he has or is likely to have under the scheme to be commuted, the order may require him to commute the whole or part of those benefits; and this section applies to the payment of any amount commuted in pursuance of the order as it applies to other payments in respect of benefits under the scheme.

25C Pensions: lump sums A8

(1) The power of the court under section 23 above to order a party to a marriage to pay a lump sum to the other party includes, where the benefits which the party with pension rights has or is likely to have under a pension scheme include any lump sum payable in respect of his death, power to make any of the following provisions by the order.

(2) The court may—

(a) if the trustees or managers of the pension scheme in question have power to determine the person to whom the sum, or any part of it, is to be paid, require them to pay the whole or part of that sum, when it becomes due, to the other party,

(b) if the party with pension rights has power to nominate the person to whom the sum, or any part of it, is to be paid, require the party with pension rights to nominate the other party in respect of the whole or part of that sum,

(c) in any other case, require the trustees or managers of the pension scheme in question to pay the whole or part of that sum, when it becomes due, for the benefit of the other party instead of to the person to whom, apart from the order, it would be paid.

(3) Any payment by the trustees or managers under an order made under section 23 above by virtue of this section shall discharge so much of the trustees' or managers' liability in respect of the party with pension rights as corresponds to the amount of the payment.

25D Pensions: supplementary   A9

(1) Where—

(a) an order made under section 23 above by virtue of section 25B or 25C above imposes any requirement on the trustees or managers of a pension scheme ("the first scheme") and the party with pension rights acquires transfer credits under another pension scheme ("the new scheme") which are derived (directly or indirectly) from a transfer from the first scheme of all his accrued rights under that scheme (including transfer credits allowed by that scheme), and

(b) the trustees or managers of the new scheme have been given notice in accordance with regulations,

the order shall have effect as if it has been made instead in respect of the trustees or managers of the new scheme; and in this subsection "transfer credits" has the same meaning as in the Pension Schemes Act 1993.

(2) Regulations may—

(a) in relation to any provision of sections 25B or 25C above which authorises the court making an order under section 23 above to require the trustees or managers of a pension scheme to make a payment for the benefit of the other party, make provision as to the person to whom, and the terms on which the payment is to be made,

(b) require notices to be given in respect of changes of circumstances relevant to such orders which include provision made by virtue of sections 25B and 25C above,

(c) make provision for the trustees or managers of any pension scheme to provide, for the purposes of orders under section 23 above, information as to the value of any benefits under the scheme,

(d) make provision for the recovery of the administrative expenses of—

   (i) complying with such orders, so far as they include provision made by virtue of sections 25B and 25C above, and

   (ii) providing such information,

   from the party with pension rights or the other party,

(e) make provision for the value of any benefits under a pension scheme to be calculated and verified, in accordance with guidance which is prepared and from time to time revised by a prescribed person and approved by the Secretary of State.

(3) In this section and sections 25B and 25C above—

(a) references to a pension scheme include—

    (i) a retirement annuity contract, or

    (ii) an annuity, or insurance policy, purchased or transferred for the purpose of giving effect to rights under a pension scheme,

(b) in relation to such a contract or annuity, references to the trustees or managers shall be read as references to the provider of the annuity,

(c) in relation to such a policy, references to the trustees or managers shall be read as references to the insurer,

and in section 25B(1) and (2) above, references to benefits under a pension scheme include any benefits by way of pension, whether under a pension scheme or not.

(4) In this section and sections 25B and 25C above—

"the party with pensions rights" means the party to the marriage who has or is likely to have benefits under a pension scheme and "the other party" means the other party to the marriage,

"pension scheme" means an occupational pension scheme or a personal pension scheme (applying the definitions in section 1 of the Pension Schemes Act 1993, but as if the reference to employed earners in the definition of "personal pension scheme" were to any earners),

"prescribed" means prescribed by regulations, and

"regulations" means regulations made by the Lord Chancellor,

and the power to make regulations under this section shall be exercisable by statutory instrument which shall be subject to annulment in pursuance of a resolution of either House of Parliament.

* * *

28 Duration of continuing financial provision orders in favour of party to marriage, and effect of remarriage   A10

(1) Subject in the case of an order made on or after the grant of a decree of a divorce or nullity of marriage to the provisions of sections 25A(2) above and 31(7) below, the term to be specified in a periodical payments or secured periodical payments order in favour of a party to a marriage shall be such term as the court thinks fit, except that the term shall not begin before or extend beyond the following limits, that is to say—

(a) in the case of a periodical payments order, the term shall begin not earlier than the date of the making of an application for the order, and shall be so defined as not to extend beyond the death of either of the parties to the marriage or, where the order is made on or after the grant of a decree of divorce or nullity of marriage, the remarriage of the party in whose favour the order is made; and

(b) in the case of a secured periodical payments order, the term shall begin not earlier than the date of the making of an application for the order, and shall be so defined as not to extend beyond the death or, where the order is made on or after the grant of such a decree, the remarriage of the party in whose favour the order is made.

(1A) Where a periodical payments or secured periodical payments order in favour of a party to a marriage is made on or after the grant of a decree of divorce or nullity of marriage, the court may direct that that party shall not be entitled to apply under section 31 below for the extension of the term specified in the order.

(2) Where a periodical payments or secured periodical payments order in favour of a party to a marriage is made otherwise than on or after the grant of a decree of divorce or nullity of marriage, and the marriage in question is subsequently dissolved or annulled but the order continues in force, the order shall, notwithstanding anything in it, cease to have effect on the remarriage of that party, except in relation to any arrears due under it on the date of the remarriage.

(3) If after the grant of a decree dissolving or annulling a marriage either party to that marriage remarries whether at any time before or after the commencement of this Act, that party shall not be entitled to apply, by reference to the grant of that decree, for a financial provision order in his or her favour, or for a property adjustment order, against the other party to that marriage.

29 Duration of continuing financial provision orders in favour of children, and age limit on making certain orders in their favour   **A11**

(1) Subject to subsection (3) below, no financial provision order and no order for a transfer of property under section 24(1)(a) above shall be made in favour of a child who has attained the age of eighteen.

(2) The term to be specified in a periodical payments or secured periodical payments order in favour of a child may begin with the date of the making of an application for the order in question or any later date or a date ascertained in accordance with subsection (5) or (6) below but—

(a) shall not in the first instance extend beyond the date of the birthday of the child next following his attaining the upper limit of the compulsory school age (construed in accordance with section 8 of the Education Act 1996) unless the court considers that in the circumstances of the case the welfare of the child requires that it should extend to a later date; and

(b) shall not in any event, subject to subsection (3) below, extend beyond the date of the child's eighteenth birthday.

(3) Subsection (1) above, and paragraph (b) of subsection (2), shall not apply in the case of a child, if it appears to the court that—

(a) the child is, or will be, or if an order were made without complying with either or both of those provisions would be, receiving instruction at an educational establishment or undergoing training for a trade, profession or vocation, whether or not he is also, or will also be, in gainful employment; or

(b) there are special circumstances which justify the making of an order without complying with either or both of those provisions.

(4) Any periodical payments order in favour of a child shall, notwithstanding anything in the order, cease to have effect on the death of the person liable to make payments under the order, except in relation to any arrears due under the order on the date of the death.

(5) Where—

(a) a maintenance assessment ("the current assessment") is in force with respect to a child; and

(b) an application is made under Part II of this Act for a periodical payments or secured periodical payments order in favour of that child—

(i) in accordance with section 8 of the Child Support Act 1991, and

(ii) before the end of the period of 6 months beginning with the making of the current assessment

the term to be specified in any such order made on that application may be expressed to begin on, or at any time after, the earliest permitted date.

(6) For the purposes of subsection (5) above, "the earliest permitted date" is whichever is the later of—

(a) the date 6 months before the application is made; or

(b) the date on which the current assessment took effect or, where successive maintenance assessments have been continuously in force with respect to a child, on which the first of those assessments took effect.

(7) Where—

(a) a maintenance assessment ceases to have effect or is cancelled by or under any provision of the Child Support Act 1991; and

(b) an application is made, before the end of the period of 6 months beginning with the relevant date, for a periodical payments or secured periodical payments order in favour of a child with respect to whom that maintenance assessment was in force immediately before it ceased to have effect or was cancelled,

the term to be specified in any such order made on that application may begin with the date on which that maintenance assessment ceased to have effect or, as the case may be, the date with effect from which it was cancelled, or any later date.

(8) In subsection (7)(b) above—

(a) where the maintenance assessment ceased to have effect, the relevant date is the date on which it so ceased; and

(b) where the maintenance assessment was cancelled, the relevant date is the later of—

(i) the date on which the person who cancelled it did so, and

(ii) the date from which the cancellation first had effect.

30 Direction for settlement of instrument for securing payments or effecting property adjustment   A12

Where the court decides to make a financial provision order requiring any payments to be secured or a property adjustment order—

(a) it may direct that the matter be referred to one of the conveyancing counsel of the court for him to settle a proper instrument to be executed by all necessary parties; and

(b) where the order is to be made in proceedings for divorce, nullity of marriage or judicial separation it may, if it thinks fit, defer the grant of the decree in question until the instrument has been duly executed.

31 Variation, discharge, etc., of certain orders for financial relief   A13

(1) Where the court has made an order to which this section applies, then subject to the provisions of this section and of section 28(1A) above, the court shall have power to vary or discharge the order or to suspend any provision thereof temporarily and to revive the operation of any provision so suspended.

(2) This section applies to the following orders, that is to say—

(a) any order for maintenance pending suit and any interim order for maintenance;

   (b) any periodical payments order;

   (c) any secured periodical payments order;

   (d) any order made by virtue of section 23(3)(c) or 27(7)(b) above (provision for payment of a lump sum by instalments);

 (dd) any deferred order made by virtue of section 23(1)(c) (lump sums) which includes provision made by virtue of—

      (i) section 25B(4), or

     (ii) section 25C,

     (provision in respect of pension rights);

   (e) any order for a settlement of property under section 24(1)(b) or for a variation of settlement under section 24(1)(c) or (d) above, being an order made on or after the grant of a decree of judicial separation;

   (f) any order made under section 24A(1) above for the sale of property.

(2A) Where the court has made an order referred to in subsection (2)(a), (b) or (c) above, then, subject to the provisions of this section, the court shall have power to remit the payment of any arrears due under the order or of any part thereof.

(2B) Where the court has made an order referred to in subsection (2)(dd)(ii) above, this section shall cease to apply to the order on the death of either of the parties to the marriage.

(3) The powers exercisable by the court under this section in relation to an order shall be exercisable also in relation to any instrument executed in pursuance of the order.

(4) The court shall not exercise the powers conferred by this section in relation to an order for a settlement under section 24(1)(b) or for a variation of settlement under section 24(1)(c) or (d) above except on an application made in proceedings—

   (a) for the rescission of the decree of judicial separation by reference to which the order was made, or

   (b) for the dissolution of the marriage in question.

(5) Subject to subsections (7A) to (7F) below and without prejudice to any power exercisable by virtue of subsection (2)(d), (dd) or (e) above or otherwise than by virtue of this section, no property adjustment order shall be made on an application for the variation of a periodical payments or secured periodical payments order made (whether in favour of a party to a marriage or in favour of a child of the family) under section 23 above, and no order for the payment of a lump sum shall be made on an application for the variation of a periodical

payments or secured periodical payments order in favour of a party to a marriage (whether made under section 23 or under section 27 above).

(6) Where the person liable to make payments under a secured periodical payments order has died, an application under this section relating to that order (and to any order made under section 24A(1) above which requires the proceeds of a sale of property to be used for securing those payments) may be made by the person entitled to payments under the periodical payments order or by the personal representatives of the deceased person, but no such application shall, except with the permission of the court, be made after the end of the period of six months from the date on which representation in regard to the estate of that person is first taken out.

(7) In exercising the powers conferred by this section the court shall have regard to all the circumstances of the case, first consideration being given to the welfare while a minor of any child of the family who has not attained the age of eighteen, and the circumstances of the case shall include any change in any of the matters to which the court was required to have regard when making the order to which the application relates, and—

(a) in the case of a periodical payments or secured periodical payments order made on or after the grant of a decree of divorce or nullity of marriage, the court shall consider whether in all the circumstances and after having regard to any such change it would be appropriate to vary the order so that payments under the order are required to be made or secured only for such further period as will in the opinion of the court be sufficient (in the light of any proposed exercise by the court, where the marriage has been dissolved, of its powers under subsection (7B) below) to enable the party in whose favour the order was made to adjust without undue hardship to the termination of those payments;

(b) in a case where the party against whom the order was made has died, the circumstances of the case shall also include the changed circumstances resulting from his or her death.

(7A) Subsection (7B) below applies where, after the dissolution of a marriage, the court—

(a) discharges a periodical payments order or secured periodical payments order made in favour of a party to the marriage; or

(b) varies such an order so that payments under the order are required to be made or secured only for such further period as is determined by the court.

(7B) The court has power, in addition to any power it has apart from this subsection, to make supplemental provision consisting of any of—

(a) an order for the payment of a lump sum in favour of a party to the marriage;

(b) one or more property adjustment orders in favour of a party to the marriage;

(c) a direction that the party in whose favour the original order discharged or varied was made is not entitled to make any further application for—

(i) a periodical payments or secured periodical payments order, or

(ii) an extension of the period to which the original order is limited by any variation made by the court.

(7C) An order for the payment of a lump sum made under subsection (7B) above may—

(a) provide for the payment of that sum by instalments of such amount as may be specified in the order; and

(b) require the payment of the instalments to be secured to the satisfaction of the court.

(7D) Section 23(6) above apply [*sic*] where the court makes an order for the payment of a lump sum under subsection (7B) above as they apply where it makes such an order under section 23 above.

(7E) If under subsection (7B) above the court makes more than one property adjustment order in favour of the same party to the marriage, each of those orders must fall within a different paragraph of section 21(2) above.

(7F) Sections 24A and 30 above apply where the court makes a property adjustment order under subsection (7B) above as they apply where it makes such an order under section 24 above.

(8) The personal representatives of a deceased person against whom a secured periodical payments order was made shall not be liable for having distributed any part of the estate of the deceased after the expiration of the period of six months referred to in subsection (6) above on the ground that they ought to have taken into account the possibility that the court might permit an application under this section to be made after that period by the person entitled to payments under the order; but this subsection shall not prejudice any power to recover any part of the estate so distributed arising by virtue of the making of an order in pursuance of this section.

(9) In considering for the purposes of subsection (6) above the question when representation was first taken out, a grant limited to settled land or to trust property shall be left out of account and a grant limited to real estate or to personal estate shall be left out of account unless a grant limited to the remainder of the estate has previously been made or is made at the same time.

(10) Where the court, in exercise of its powers under this section, decides to vary or discharge a periodical payments or secured periodical payments order,

then, subject to section 28(1) and (2) above, the court shall have power to direct that the variation or discharge shall not take effect until the expiration of such period as may be specified in the order.

(11) Where—

(a) a periodical payments or secured periodical payments order in favour of more than one child ("the order") is in force;

(b) the order requires payments specified in it to be made to or for the benefit of more than one child without apportioning those payments between them;

(c) a maintenance assessment ("the assessment") is made with respect to one or more, but not all, of the children with respect to whom those payments are to be made; and

(d) an application is made, before the end of the period of 6 months beginning with the date on which the assessment was made, for the variation or discharge of the order,

the court may, in exercise of its powers under this section to vary or discharge the order, direct that the variation or discharge shall take effect from the date on which the assessment took effect or any later date.

(12) Where—

(a) an order ("the child order") of a kind prescribed for the purposes of section 10(1) of the Child Support Act 1991 is affected by a maintenance assessment;

(b) on the date on which the child order became so affected there was in force a periodical payments or secured periodical payments order ("the spousal order") in favour of a party to a marriage having the care of the child in whose favour the child order was made; and

(c) an application is made, before the end of the period of 6 months beginning with the date on which the maintenance assessment was made, for the spousal order to be varied or discharged,

the court may, in exercise of its powers under this section to vary or discharge the spousal order, direct that the variation or discharge shall take effect from the date on which the child order became so affected or any later date.

(13) For the purposes of subsection (12) above, an order is affected if it ceases to have effect or is modified by or under section 10 of the Child Support Act 1991.

(14) Subsections (11) and (12) above are without prejudice to any other power of the court to direct that the variation or discharge of an order under this section

shall take effect from a date earlier than that on which the order for variation or discharge was made.

* * *

32 Payment of certain arrears unenforceable without the leave of the court   A14

(1) A person shall not be entitled to enforce through the High Court or any county court the payment of any arrears due under an order for maintenance pending suit, an interim order for maintenance or any financial provision order without the leave of that court if those arrears became due more than twelve months before proceedings to enforce the payment of them are begun.

(2) The court hearing an application for the grant of leave under this section may refuse leave, or may grant leave subject to such restrictions and conditions (including conditions as to the allowing of time for payment or the making of payment by instalments) as that court thinks proper, or may remit the payment of the arrears or of any part thereof.

(3) An application for the grant of leave under this section shall be made in such manner as may be prescribed by rules of court.

* * *

33A Consent orders for financial provision on property adjustment   A15

(1) Notwithstanding anything in the preceding provisions of this Part of this Act, on an application for a consent order for financial relief the court may, unless it has reason to think that there are other circumstances into which it ought to inquire, make an order in the terms agreed on the basis only of the prescribed information furnished with the application.

(2) Subsection (1) above applies to an application for a consent order varying or discharging an order for financial relief as it applies to an application for an order for financial relief.

(3) In this section—

"consent order", in relation to an application for an order, means an order in the terms applied for to which the respondent agrees;

"order for financial relief" means an order under any of sections 23, 24, 24A or 27 above; and "prescribed" means prescribed by rules of court.

* * *

37 Avoidance of transactions intended to prevent or reduce financial relief   A16

(1) For the purposes of this section "financial relief" means relief under any of the provisions of sections 22, 23, 24, 27, 31 (except subsection (6)) and 35 above, and any reference in this section to defeating a person's claim for financial relief is a reference to preventing financial relief from being granted to that person, or to that person for the benefit of a child of the family, or reducing the amount of any financial relief which might be so granted, or frustrating or impeding the enforcement of any order which might be or has been made at his instance under any of those provisions.

(2) Where proceedings for financial relief are brought by one person against another, the court may, on the application of the first-mentioned person—

(a) if it is satisfied that the other party to the proceedings is, with the intention of defeating the claim for financial relief, about to make any disposition or to transfer out of the jurisdiction or otherwise deal with any property, make such order as it thinks fit for restraining the other party from so doing or otherwise for protecting the claim;

(b) if it is satisfied that the other party has, with that intention, made a reviewable disposition and that if the disposition were set aside financial relief or different financial relief would be granted to the applicant, make an order setting aside the disposition;

(c) if it is satisfied, in a case where an order has been obtained under any of the provisions mentioned in subsection (1) above by the applicant against the other party, that the other party has, with that intention, made a reviewable disposition, make an order setting aside the disposition;

and an application for the purposes of paragraph (b) above shall be made in the proceedings for the financial relief in question.

(3) Where the court makes an order under subsection (2)(b) or (c) above setting aside a disposition it shall give such consequential directions as it thinks fit for giving effect to the order (including directions requiring the making of any payments or the disposal of any property).

(4) Any disposition made by the other party to the proceedings for financial relief in question (whether before or after the commencement of those proceedings) is a reviewable disposition for the purposes of subsection (2)(b) and (c)

above unless it was made for valuable consideration (other than marriage) to a person who, at the time of the disposition, acted in relation to it in good faith and without notice of any intention on the part of the other party to defeat the applicant's claim for financial relief.

(5) Where an application is made under this section with respect to a disposition which took place less than three years before the date of the application or with respect to a disposition or other dealing with property which is about to take place and the court is satisfied—

(a) in a case falling within subsection (2)(a) or (b) above, that the disposition or other dealing would (apart from this section) have the consequence or,

(b) in a case falling within subsection (2)(c) above, that the disposition has had the consequence,

of defeating the applicant's claim for financial relief, it shall be presumed, unless the contrary is shown, that the person who disposed of or is about to dispose of or deal with the property did so or, as the case may be, is about to do so, with the intention of defeating the applicant's claim for financial relief.

(6) In this section "disposition" does not include any provision contained in a will or codicil but, with that exception, includes any conveyance, assurance or gift of property of any description, whether made by an instrument or otherwise.

(7) This section does not apply to a disposition made before 1st January 1968.

A(b) Family Proceedings Rules 1991

Rules 2.51A to 2.70

A20 [*The rules printed below in regular type incorporate all amendments up to and including the Family Proceedings (Amendment No. 2) Rules 1999, in force from June 5, 2000. However, rule 20 of those Rules retains the earlier rules for proceedings under Part III of the 1991 Rules, i.e. applications for relief under the Married Women's Property Act, for failure to maintain, for alteration of maintenance agreements and for financial relief after foreign proceedings. The relevant earlier rules are printed in italics.*]

Application of ancillary relief rules   A21

2.51A (1) The procedures set out in rules 2.51B to 2.70 ("the ancillary relief rules") apply to any ancillary relief application and to any application under section 10(2) of the Act of 1973.

(2) In the ancillary relief rules, unless the context requires otherwise—

"applicant" means the party applying for ancillary relief;

"respondent" means the respondent to the application for ancillary relief;

"FDR appointment" means a Financial Dispute Resolution appointment in accordance with rule 2.61E.

The overriding objective   A22

2.51B (1) The ancillary relief rules are a procedural code with the overriding objective of enabling the court to deal with cases justly.

(2) Dealing with a case justly includes, so far as is practicable—

(a) ensuring that the parties are on an equal footing;

(b) saving expense;

(c) dealing with the case in ways which are proportionate—

    (i) to the amount of money involved;
    (ii) to the importance of the case;
    (iii) to the complexity of the issues; and
    (iv) to the financial position of each party;

(d) ensuring that it is dealt with expeditiously and fairly; and

(e) allotting to it an appropriate share of the court's resources, while taking into account the need to allot resources to other cases.

(3) The court must seek to give effect to the overriding objective when it—

(a) exercises any power given to it by the ancillary relief rules; or

(b) interprets any rule.

(4) The parties are required to help the court to further the overriding objective.

(5) The court must further the overriding objective by actively managing cases.

(6) Active case management includes—

(a) encouraging the parties to co-operate with each other in the conduct of the proceedings;

(b) encouraging the parties to settle their disputes through mediation, where appropriate;

(c) identifying the issues at an early date;

(d) regulating the extent of disclosure of documents and expert evidence so that they are proportionate to the issues in question;

(e) helping the parties to settle the whole or part of the case;

(f) fixing timetables or otherwise controlling the progress of the case;

(g) making use of technology; and

(h) giving directions to ensure that the trial of a case proceeds quickly and efficiently.

Right to be heard on ancillary questions   A23

2.52 A respondent may be heard on any question of ancillary relief without filing an answer and whether or not he has returned to the court office an acknowledgement of service stating his wish to be heard on that question.

Application by petitioner or respondent for ancillary relief   A24

2.53 (1) Any application by a petitioner, or by a respondent who files an answer claiming relief, for—

(a) an order for maintenance pending suit,

22

(b) a financial provision order,

(c) a property adjustment order,

shall be made in the petition or answer, as the case may be.

(2) Notwithstanding anything in paragraph (1), an application for ancillary relief which should have been made in the petition or answer may be made subsequently—

(a) by leave of the court, either by notice in Form A or at the trial, or

(b) where the parties are agreed upon the terms of the proposed order, without leave by notice in Form A.

(3) An application by a petitioner or respondent for ancillary relief, not being an application which is required to be made in the petition or answer, shall be made by notice in Form A.

Application by parent, guardian etc. for ancillary relief in respect of children   A25

2.54 (1) Any of the following persons, namely—

(a) a parent or guardian of any child of the family,

(b) any person in whose favour a residence order has been made with respect to a child of the family, and any applicant for such an order,

(c) any other person who is entitled to apply for a residence order with respect to a child,

(d) a local authority, where an order has been made under section 30(1)(a) of the Act of 1989 placing a child in its care,

(e) the Official Solicitor, if appointed the guardian ad litem of a child of a family under rule 9.5, and

(f) a child of a family who has been given leave to intervene in the cause for the purpose of applying for ancillary relief,

may apply for an order for ancillary relief as respects that child by notice in Form A.

(2) In this rule "residence order" has the meaning assigned to it by section 8(1) of the Act of 1989.

2.55 [*repealed*]

2.56 [*repealed*]

Children to be separately represented on certain applications   A26

2.57 (1) Where an application is made to the High Court or a divorce county court for an order for a variation of settlement, the court shall, unless it is satisfied that the proposed variation does not adversely affect the rights or interests of any children concerned, direct that the children be separately represented on the application, either by a solicitor or by a solicitor and counsel, and may appoint the Official Solicitor or other fit person to be guardian ad litem of the children for the purpose of the application.

(2) On any other application for ancillary relief the court may give such a direction or make such appointment as it is empowered to give or make by paragraph (1).

(3) Before a person other than the Official Solicitor is appointed guardian ad litem under this rule there shall be filed a certificate by the solicitor acting for the children that the person proposed as guardian has no interest in the matter adverse to that of the children and that he is a proper person to be such guardian.

2.58 [*repealed*]

Evidence on application for property adjustment or avoidance of disposition order   A27

2.59 [*(1) Where an application is made for a property adjustment order or an avoidance of disposition order, the affidavit in support shall contain, so far as known to the applicant, full particulars—*

(a) in the case of an application for a transfer or settlement of property—

    (i) of the property in respect of which the application is made,

    (ii) of the property to which the party against whom the application is made is entitled either in possession or reversion;

(b) in the case of an application for an order for a variation of settlement—

    (i) of all settlements, whether ante-nuptial or post-nuptial, made on the spouses, and

    (ii) of the funds brought into settlement by each spouse;

(c) in the case of an application for an avoidance of disposition order—

    (i) of the property to which the disposition relates,

> *(ii) of the person in whose favour the disposition is alleged to have been made, and in the case of a disposition alleged to have been made by way of settlement, of the trustees and the beneficiaries of the settlement.]*

(2) Where an application for a property adjustment order or an avoidance of disposition order relates to land, the notice in [Form A] [*Form M11 or M13*] shall identify the land and—

(a) state whether the title to the land is registered or unregistered and, if registered, the Land Registry title number; and

(b) give particulars, so far as known to the applicant, of any mortgage of the land or any interest therein.

(3) [Copies of Form A and of Form E completed by the applicant] [*A copy of Form M11 or M13 as the case may be, together with a copy of the supporting affidavit,*] shall be served on the following persons as well as on the respondent to the application, that is to say—

(a) in the case of an application for an order for a variation of settlement, the trustees of the settlement and the settlor if living;

(b) in the case of an application for an avoidance of disposition order, the person in whose favour the disposition is alleged to have been made;

and such other persons, if any, as the district judge may direct.

(4) In the case of an application to which paragraph (2) refers, a copy of [Form A] [*Form M11 or M13 as the case may be*] shall be served on any mortgagee of whom particulars are given pursuant to that paragraph; any person so served may apply to the court in writing, within 14 days after service, for a copy of the applicant's [Form E] [*affidavit*].

(5) Any person who—

(a) is served with [copies of Forms A and E] [*an affidavit*] pursuant to paragraph (3), or

(b) receives [a copy of Form E] [*an affidavit*] following an application made in accordance with paragraph (4),

may, within 14 days after service or receipt, as the case may be, file [a statement] [*an affidavit*] in answer.

(6) A statement filed under paragraph (5) shall be sworn to be true.

[Service of statement in answer

2.60 (1) Where a form or other document filed with the court contains an allegation of adultery or of an improper association with a named person ("the named person"), the court may direct that the party who filed the relevant form or document serve a copy of all or part of that form or document on the named person, together with Form F.

(2) If the court makes a direction under paragraph (1), the named person may file a statement in answer to the allegations.

(3) A statement under paragraph (2) shall be sworn to be true.

(4) Rule 2.37(3) shall apply to a person served under paragraph (1) as it applies to a co-respondent.]

[*Service of affidavit in answer or reply*

2.60 *(1) A person who files an affidavit for use on an application under rule 2.58 or 2.59 shall at the same time serve a copy on the opposite party and, where the affidavit contains an allegation of adultery or of an improper association with a named person, then, if the court so directs, it shall be endorsed with a notice in Form M14 and a copy of the affidavit or of such part thereof as the court may direct, indorsed as aforesaid, shall be served on that person by the person who files the affidavit, and the person against whom the allegation is made shall be entitled to intervene in the proceedings by applying for directions under rule 2.62(5) within seven days of service of the affidavit on him.*

(2) Rule 2.37(3) shall apply to a person served with an affidavit under paragraph (1) of this rule as it applies to a co-respondent.]

Information on application for consent order for financial relief   A28

2.61 (1) Subject to paragraphs (2) and (3), there shall be lodged with every application for a consent order under any of sections 23, 24 or 24A of the Act of 1973 two copies of a draft of the order in the terms sought, one of which shall be indorsed with a statement signed by the respondent to the application signifying his agreement, and a statement of information (which may be made in more than one document) which shall include—

    (a) the duration of the marriage, the age of each party and of any minor or dependent child of the family;

(b) an estimate in summary form of the approximate amount or value of the capital resources and net income of each party and of any minor child of the family;

(c) what arrangements are intended for the accommodation for each of the parties and any minor child of the family;

(d) whether either party has remarried or has any present intention to marry or to cohabit with another person;

(dd) where the order imposes any requirement on the trustees or managers of a pension scheme by virtue of section 25B or 25C of the Act of 1973, a statement confirming that those trustees or managers have been served with notice of the application and that no objection to such an order has been made by them within 14 days from such service;

(e) where the terms of the order provide for a transfer of property, a statement confirming that any mortgagee of that property has been served with notice of the application and that no objection to such a transfer has been made by the mortgagee within 14 days from such service; and

(f) any other especially significant matters.

(2) Where an application is made for a consent order varying an order for periodical payments paragraph (1) shall be sufficiently complied with if the statement of information required to be lodged with the application includes only the information in respect of net income mentioned in paragraph (1)(b) (and, where appropriate, a statement under paragraph (1)(dd)), and an application for a consent order for interim periodical payments pending the determination of an application for ancillary relief may be made in like manner.

(3) Where all or any of the parties attend the hearing of an application for financial relief the court may dispense with the lodging of a statement of information in accordance with paragraph (1) and give directions for the information which would otherwise be required to be given in such a statement to be given in such a manner as it sees fit.

Application for ancillary relief   A29

2.61A (1) A notice of intention to proceed with an application for ancillary relief made in the petition or answer or an application for ancillary relief must be made by notice in Form A.

(2) The notice must be filed:

(a) if the case is pending in a divorce county court, in that court; or

(b) if the case is pending in the High Court, in the registry in which it is proceeding.

(3) Where the applicant requests an order for ancillary relief that includes provision to be made by virtue of section 25B or 25C of the Act of 1973 the terms of the order requested must be specified in the notice in Form A.

(4) Upon the filing of Form A the court must:

(a) fix a first appointment not less than 12 weeks and not more than 16 weeks after the date of the filing of the notice and give notice of that date;

(b) serve a copy on the respondent within 4 days of the date of the filing of the notice.

(5) The date fixed under paragraph (4) for the first appointment, or for any subsequent appointment, must not be cancelled except with the court's permission and, if cancelled, the court must immediately fix a new date.

Procedure before the first appointment   A30

2.61B (1) Both parties must, at the same time, exchange with each other, and each file with the court, a statement in Form E, which—

(a) is signed by the party who made the statement;

(b) is sworn to be true; and

(c) contains the information and has attached to it the documents required by that Form.

(2) Form E must be exchanged and filed not less than 35 days before the date of the first appointment.

(3) Form E must have attached to it:

(a) any documents required by Form E; and

(b) any other documents necessary to explain or clarify any of the information contained in Form E.

(4) Form E must have no documents attached to it other than the documents referred to in paragraph (3).

(5) Where a party was unavoidably prevented from sending any document required by Form E, that party must at the earliest opportunity:

(a) serve copies of that document on the other party; and

(b) file a copy of that document with the court, together with a statement explaining the failure to send it with Form E.

(6) No disclosure or inspection of documents may be requested or given between the filing of the application for ancillary relief and the first appointment, except—

(a) copies sent with Form E, or in accordance with paragraph (5); or

(b) in accordance with paragraph (7).

(7) At least 14 days before the hearing of the first appointment, each party must file with the court and serve on the other party—

(a) a concise statement of the issues between the parties;

(b) a chronology;

(c) a questionnaire setting out by reference to the concise statement of issues any further information and documents requested from the other party or a statement that no information and documents are required;

(d) a notice in Form G stating whether that party will be in a position at the first appointment to proceed on that occasion to a FDR appointment.

(8) Where an order for ancillary relief is requested that includes provision to be made under section 25B or 25C of the Act of 1973, the applicant must file with the court and serve on the respondent at least 14 days before the hearing of the first appointment, confirmation that rule 2.70(4) has been complied with.

(9) At least 14 days before the hearing of the first appointment the applicant must file with the court and serve on the respondent, confirmation of the names of all persons served in accordance with rule 2.59(3) and (4), and that there are no other persons who must be served in accordance with those paragraphs.

Expert evidence   A31

2.61C CPR rules 35.1 to 35.14 relating to expert evidence (with appropriate modifications), except CPR rules 35.5(2) and 35.8(4)(b), apply to all ancillary relief proceedings.

The first appointment   A32

2.61D (1) The first appointment must be conducted with the objective of defining the issues and saving costs.

(2) At the first appointment the district judge—

(a) must determine—

    (i) the extent to which any questions seeking information under rule 2.61B must be answered; and

    (ii) what documents requested under rule 2.61B must be produced,

and give directions for the production of such further documents as may be necessary;

(b) must give directions about—

    (i) the valuation of assets (including, where appropriate, the joint instruction of joint experts);

    (ii) obtaining and exchanging expert evidence, if required; and

    (iii) evidence to be adduced by each party and, where appropriate, about further chronologies or schedules to be filed by each party;

(c) must, unless he decides that a referral is not appropriate in the circumstances, direct that the case be referred to a FDR appointment;

(d) must, where he decides that a referral to a FDR appointment is not appropriate, direct one of the following—

    (i) that a further directions appointment be fixed;

    (ii) that an appointment be fixed for the making of an interim order;

    (iii) that the case be fixed for final hearing and, where that direction is given, the district judge must determine the judicial level at which the case should be heard; or

    (iv) that the case be adjourned for out-of-court mediation or private negotiation or, in exceptional circumstances, generally;

(e) must consider whether, having regard to all the circumstances (including the extent to which each party has complied with this Part, and in particular the requirement to send documents with Form E), to make an order about the costs of the hearing; and

(f) may—

    (i) make an interim order where an application for it has been made in accordance with rule 2.69F returnable at the first appointment;

    (ii) having regard to the contents of Form G filed by the parties, treat the appointment (or part of it) as a FDR appointment to which rule 2.61E applies;

    (iii) in a case where an order for ancillary relief is requested that includes provision to be made under section 25B or 25C of the Act of 1973, require any party to request a valuation under regulation 4 of the Divorce etc. (Pensions) Regulations 1996 from the trustees or managers of any pension scheme under which the party has, or is likely to have, any benefits.

(3) After the first appointment, a party is not entitled to production of any further documents except in accordance with directions given under paragraph (2)(a) above or with the permission of the court.

(4) At any stage:

(a) a party may apply for further directions or a FDR appointment;

(b) the court may give further directions or direct that the parties attend a FDR appointment.

(5) Both parties must personally attend the first appointment unless the court orders otherwise.

The FDR appointment   A33

2.61E (1) The FDR appointment must be treated as a meeting held for the purposes of discussion and negotiation and paragraphs (2) to (9) apply.

(2) The district judge or judge hearing the FDR appointment must have no further involvement with the application, other than to conduct any further FDR appointment or to make a consent order or a further directions order.

(3) Not later than 7 days before the FDR appointment, the applicant must file with the court details of all offers and proposals, and responses to them.

(4) Paragraph (3) includes any offers, proposals or responses made wholly or partly without prejudice, but paragraph (3) does not make any material admissible as evidence if, but for that paragraph, it would not be admissible.

(5) At the conclusion of the FDR appointment, any documents filed under paragraph (3), and any filed documents referring to them, must, at the request of the party who filed them, be returned to him and not retained on the court file.

(6) Parties attending the FDR appointment must use their best endeavours to reach agreement on the matters in issue between them.

(7) The FDR appointment may be adjourned from time to time.

(8) At the conclusion of the FDR appointment, the court may make an appropriate consent order, but otherwise must give directions for the future course of the proceedings, including, where appropriate, the filing of evidence and fixing a final hearing date.

(9) Both parties must personally attend the FDR appointment unless the court orders otherwise.

Costs   A34

2.61F (1) At every court hearing or appointment each party must produce to the court an estimate in Form H of the costs incurred by him up to the date of that hearing or appointment.

(2) The parties' obligation under paragraph (1) is without prejudice to their obligations under paragraphs 4.1 to 4.11 of the Practice Direction relating to CPR Part 44.

Investigation by district judge of application for ancillary relief   A35

2.62 [*(1) On or after the filing of a notice in Form M11 or M13 an appointment shall be fixed for the hearing of the application by the district judge.*]

(2) An application for an avoidance of disposition order shall, if practicable, be heard at the same time as any related application for financial relief.

[*(3) Notice of the appointment, unless given in Form M11 or M13 (as the case may be), shall be given by the proper officer to every party to the application.*]

(4) At the hearing of an application for ancillary relief the district judge shall, subject to rules 2.64, 2.65 and 10.10 investigate the allegations made in support of and in answer to the application, and may take evidence orally and may at any stage of the proceedings, whether before or during the hearing, order the attendance of any person for the purpose of being examined or cross-examined and order the [disclosure and inspection] [*discovery and production*] of any document or require further [statements] [*affidavits*].

(4A) A statement filed under paragraph (4) shall be sworn to be true.

[*(5) The district judge may at any stage of the proceedings give directions as to the filing and service of pleadings and as to the further conduct of the proceedings.*

(6) Where any party to such an application intends on the day appointed for the hearing to apply for directions, he shall file and serve on every other party a notice to that effect.]

(7) Any party may apply to the court for an order that any person do attend an appointment [(an "inspection appointment")] [*(a "production appointment")*] before the court and produce any documents to be specified or described in the order, the [inspection] [*production*] of which appears to the court to be necessary for disposing fairly of the application for ancillary relief or for saving costs.

(8) No person shall be compelled by an order under paragraph (7) to produce any document at [an inspection] [*a production*] appointment which he could not be compelled to produce at the hearing of the application for ancillary relief.

(9) The court shall permit any person attending [an inspection] [*a production*] appointment pursuant to an order under paragraph (7) above to be represented at the appointment.

[Request for further information etc.   A36

2.63 *Any party to an application for ancillary relief may by letter require any other party to give further information concerning any matter contained in any affidavit filed by or on behalf of that other party or any other relevant matter, or to furnish a list of relevant documents or to allow inspection of any such document, and may, in default of compliance by such other party, apply to the district judge for directions.*]

Order on application for ancillary relief   A37

2.64 (1) Subject to rule 2.65 the district judge shall, after completing his investigation under rule 2.62, make such order as he thinks just.

(2) Pending the final determination of the application [and subject to rule 2.69F], the district judge may make an interim order upon such terms as he thinks just.

(3) RSC Order 31, rule 1 (power to order sale of land) shall apply to applications for ancillary relief as it applies to causes and matters in the Chancery Division.

Reference of application to judge   A38

2.65 The district judge may at any time refer an application for ancillary relief, or any question arising thereon, to a judge for his decision.

Arrangements for hearing of application etc. by judge   A39

2.66 (1) Where an application for ancillary relief or any question arising thereon has been referred or adjourned to a judge, the proper officer shall fix a date, time and place for the hearing of the application or the consideration of the question and give notice thereof to all parties.

(2) The hearing or consideration shall, unless the court otherwise directs, take place in chambers.

(3) Where the application is proceeding in a divorce county court which is not a court of trial or is pending in the High Court and proceeding in a district registry which is not in a divorce town, the hearing or consideration shall take place at such court of trial or divorce town as in the opinion of the district judge is the nearest or most convenient. For the purpose of this paragraph the Royal Courts of Justice shall be treated as a divorce town.

(4) In respect of any application referred to him under this rule, a judge shall have the same powers [to make directions as a district judge has under these rules] [*as a district judge has under rule 2.62(5)*].

Request for periodical payments order at same rate as order for maintenance pending suit A40

2.67 (1) Where at or after the date of a decree nisi of divorce or nullity of marriage an order for maintenance pending suit is in force, the party in whose favour the order was made may, if he has made an application for an order for periodical payments for himself in his petition or answer, as the case may be, request the district judge in writing to make such an order (in this rule referred to as a "corresponding order") providing for payments at the same rate as those provided for by the order for maintenance pending suit.

(2) Where such a request is made, the proper officer shall serve on the other spouse a notice in Form I requiring him, if he objects to the making of a corresponding order, to give notice to that effect to the court and to the applicant within 14 days after service of the notice in Form I.

(3) If the other spouse does not give notice of objection within the time aforesaid, the district judge may make a corresponding order without further notice to that spouse and without requiring the attendance of the applicant or his solicitor, and shall in that case serve a copy of the order on the applicant as well as on the other spouse.

Application for order under section 37(2)(a) of Act of 1973 A41

2.68 (1) An application under section 37(2)(a) of the Act of 1973 for an order restraining any person from attempting to defeat a claim for financial provision or otherwise for protecting the claim may be made to the district judge.

(2) Rules 2.65 and 2.66 shall apply, with the necessary modifications, to the application as if it were an application for ancillary relief.

Offers to settle A42

2.69 (1) Either party to the application may at any time make a written offer to the other party which is expressed to be "without prejudice except as to costs" and which relates to any issue in the proceedings relating to the application.

(2) Where an offer is made under paragraph (1), the fact that such an offer has been made shall not be communicated to the court, except in accordance with rule 2.61E(3), until the question of costs falls to be decided.

Interpretation of rules 2.69B to 2.69D A43

2.69A (1) In rule 2.69B to 2.69D, "base rate" has the same meaning as in the Civil Procedure Rules 1998.

Judgment or order more advantageous than an offer made by the other party A44

2.69B (1) This rule applies where the judgment or order in favour of the applicant or respondent is more advantageous to him than an offer made under rule 2.69(1) by the other party.

(2) The court must, unless it considers it unjust to do so, order that other party to pay any costs incurred after the date beginning 28 days after the offer was made.

Judgment or order more advantageous than offers made by both parties A45

2.69C (1) This rules applies where

(a) both the applicant and the respondent have made offers under rule 2.69(1); and

(b) the judgment or order in favour of the applicant or the respondent, as the case may be, is more advantageous to him than both of the offers referred to in paragraph (a).

(2) The court may, where it considers it just, order interest in accordance with paragraph (3) on the whole or part of any sum of money (excluding interest and periodical payments) to be awarded to the applicant or respondent, as the case may be.

35

(3) Interest under paragraph (2) may be at a rate not exceeding 10% above base rate for some or all of the period beginning 28 days after the offer was made.

(4) The court may also order that the applicant or respondent, as the case may be, is entitled to:

    (a) his costs on the indemnity basis beginning 28 days after the offer was made; and

    (b) interest on those costs at a rate not exceeding 10% above base rate.

(5) The court's powers under this rule are in addition to its powers under rule 2.69B.

Factors for court's consideration under rules 2.69B and 2.69C   A46

2.69D (1) In considering whether it would be unjust, or whether it would be just, to make the orders referred to in rules 2.69B and 2.69C, the court must take into account all the circumstances of the case, including—

    (a) the terms of any offers made under rule 2.69(1);

    (b) the stage in the proceedings when any offer was made;

    (c) the information available to the parties at the time when the offer was made;

    (d) the conduct of the parties with regard to the giving or refusing to give information for the purposes of enabling the offer to be made or evaluated; and

    (e) the respective means of the parties.

(2) The power of the court to award interest under rule 2.69C(2) and (4)(b) is in addition to any other power it may have to award interest.

Open proposals   A47

2.69E (1) Not less than 14 days before the date fixed for the final hearing of an application for ancillary relief, the applicant must (unless the court directs otherwise) file with the court and serve on the respondent an open statement which sets out concise details, including the amounts involved, of the orders which he proposes to ask the court to make.

(2) Not more than 7 days after service of a statement under paragraph (1), the respondent must file with the court and serve on the applicant an open statement

which sets out concise details, including the amounts involved, of the orders which he proposes to ask the court to make.

Application for interim orders   A48

2.69F (1) A party may apply at any stage of the proceedings for an order for maintenance pending suit, interim periodical payments or an interim variation order.

(2) An application for such an order must be made by notice of application and the date fixed for the hearing of the application must be not less than 14 days after the date the notice of application is issued.

(3) The applicant shall forthwith serve the respondent with a copy of the notice of application.

(4) Where an application is made before a party has filed Form E, that party must file with the application and serve on the other party, a draft of the order requested and a short sworn statement explaining why the order is necessary and giving the necessary information about his means.

(5) Not less than 7 days before the date fixed for the hearing, the respondent must file with the court and serve on the other party, a short sworn statement about his means, unless he has already filed Form E.

(6) A party may apply for any other form of interim order at any stage of the proceedings with or without notice.

(7) Where an application referred to in paragraph (6) is made with notice, the provisions of paragraphs (1) to (5) apply to it.

(8) Where an application referred to in paragraph (6) is made without notice, the provisions of paragraph (1) apply to it.

Pensions   A49

2.70 (1) [*repealed*]

(2) Where by virtue of rule 2.62(4) the district judge has power to order [disclosure] [*discovery*] of any document, he shall also have power to require either party to request a valuation under regulation 4 from the trustees or managers of any pension scheme under which that party has or is likely to have any benefits.

(3) No order including provision made by virtue of section 25B or 25C of the Act of 1973 shall be made unless such provision has been sought by way of—

(a) Form A in accordance with rule 2.61A; or

(b) [*repealed*]

(c) a draft order lodged in accordance with rule 2.61.

(4) Where an application is made for an order which by virtue of section 25B or 25C of the Act of 1973 imposes any requirement on the trustees or managers of a pension scheme, a copy of Form A shall be served on those trustees or managers together with the following:

(a) an address to which any notice which the trustees or managers are required to serve under the Divorce etc. (Pensions) Regulations 1996 is to be sent;

(b) an address to which any payment which the trustees or managers are required to make to the applicant is to be sent; and

(c) where the address in sub-paragraph (b) is that of a bank, a building society or the Department of National Savings, sufficient details to enable payment to be made into the account of the applicant.

(5) Trustees or managers of a pension scheme on whom a copy of such a notice is served may, within 14 days after service, require the applicant to provide them with a copy of the affidavit supporting his application.

(6) Trustees or managers of a pension scheme who receive a copy of an affidavit as required pursuant to paragraph (5) may within 14 days after receipt file an affidavit in answer.

(7) Trustees or managers of a pension scheme who file an affidavit pursuant to paragraph (6) may file therewith a notice to the court requiring an appointment to be fixed; and where such a notice is filed

(a) the proper officer shall fix an appointment for the hearing or further hearing of the application and give not less than 14 days' notice of that appointment to the petitioner, the respondent and the trustees or managers of the pension scheme; and

(b) the trustees or managers of the pension scheme shall be entitled to be represented at any such hearing.

(8) Where the petitioner and respondent have agreed on the terms of an order which by virtue of section 25B or 25C of the Act of 1973 imposes any requirement on the trustees or managers of a pension scheme, then unless service has already been effected under paragraph (4), they shall serve on the trustees or managers notice of the application together with the particulars set out in sub-paragraphs (a), (b) and (c) of paragraph (4), and no such order shall be made unless either

(a) the trustees or managers have not made any objection within 14 days after the service on them of such notice; or

(b) the court has considered the objection made by the trustees or managers

and for the purpose of considering any such objection the court may make such direction as it sees fit for the trustees or managers to attend before it or to furnish written details of their objection.

(9) Upon the making, amendment or revocation of an order which by virtue of section 25B or 25C of the Act of 1973 imposes any requirement on the trustees or managers of a pension scheme, the party in whose favour the order is or was made shall serve a copy of that order, or as the case may be of the order amending or revoking that order, upon the trustees or managers.

(10) In this rule—

(a) every reference to a regulation by number alone means the regulation so numbered in the Divorce etc. (Pensions) Regulations 1996;

(b) all words and phrases defined in section 25D(3) and (4) of the Act of 1973 have the meanings assigned by those sub-sections.

A(c) President's Direction, January 31, 1995 (case management)

A70 1. The importance of reducing the cost and delay of civil litigation makes it necessary for the Court to assert greater control over the preparation for and conduct of hearings than has hitherto been customary. Failure by practitioners to conduct cases economically will be visited by appropriate orders for costs, including wasted costs orders.

2. The Court will accordingly exercise its discretion to limit—

(a) discovery;

(b) the length of opening and closing oral submissions;

(c) the time allowed for the examination and cross-examination of witnesses;

(d) the issues on which it wishes to be addressed;

(e) reading aloud from documents and authorities.

3. Unless otherwise ordered, every witness statement or affidavit shall stand as the evidence in chief of the witness concerned. The substance of the evidence which a party intends to adduce at the hearing must be sufficiently detailed, but without prolixity; it must be confined to material matters of fact, not (except in the case of the evidence of professional witnesses) of opinion; and if hearsay evidence is to be adduced, the source of the information must be declared or good reason given for not doing so.

4. It is a duty owed to the court both by the parties and by their legal representatives to give full and frank disclosure in ancillary relief applications and also in all matters in respect of children. The parties and their advisers must also use their best endeavours:

(a) to confine the issues and the evidence called to what is reasonably considered to be essential for the proper presentation of their case;

(b) to reduce or eliminate issues for expert evidence;

(c) in advance of the hearing to agree which are the issues or the main issues.

5. [*Deleted by President's Direction, March 10, 2000. See precedent B1(d).*]

6. In cases estimated to last for 5 days or more and in which no pre-trial review has been ordered, application should be made for a pre-trial review. It should when practicable be listed at least 3 weeks before the hearing and be conducted by the judge or district judge before whom the case is to be heard and should be

attended by the advocates who are to represent the parties at the hearing. Whenever possible, all statements of evidence and all reports should be filed before the date of the review and in good time for them to have been considered by all parties.

7. Whenever practicable and in any matter estimated to last 5 days or more, each party should, not less than 2 clear days before the hearing, lodge with the Court, or the Clerk of the Rules in matters in the RCJ in London, and deliver to other parties, a chronology and a skeleton argument concisely summarising that party's submissions in relation to each of the issues, and citing the main authorities relied upon. It is important that skeleton arguments should be brief.

8. [*Deleted by President's Direction, March 10, 2000. See precedent B1(d).*]

9. The opening speech should be succinct. At its conclusion other parties may be invited briefly to amplify their skeleton arguments. In a heavy case the Court may in conjunction with final speeches require written submissions, including the findings of fact for which each party contends.

10. This Practice Direction which follows the directions handed down by the Lord Chief Justice and the Vice-Chancellor to apply in the Queen's Bench and Chancery Divisions, shall apply to all family proceedings in the High Court and in all Care Centres, Family Hearing Centres and divorce county courts.

11. Issued with the concurrence of the Lord Chancellor.

A(d) President's Direction, March 10, 2000 (bundles)

A70 1. The following practice applies to all hearings in family proceedings in the High Court, to all hearings of family proceedings in the Royal Courts of Justice and to hearings with a time estimate of half a day or more in all care centres, family hearing centres and divorce county courts (including the Principal Registry of the Family Division when so treated), except as specified in paragraph 2.3 below, and subject to specific directions given in any particular case. "Hearing" extends to all hearings before judges and district judges and includes the hearing of any application.

2.1 A bundle for the use of the court at the hearing shall be provided by the party in the position of applicant at the hearing or by any other party who agrees to do so. It shall contain copies of all documents relevant to the hearing in chronological order, paginated and indexed and divided into separate sections, as follows:

(a) applications and orders;

(b) statements and affidavits;

(c) experts' reports and other reports including those of a guardian ad litem; and

(d) other documents, divided into further sections as may be appropriate.

2.2 Where the nature of the hearing is such that a complete bundle of all documents is unnecessary, the bundle may comprise only those documents necessary for the hearing but the summary (paragraph 3.1(a) below) must commence with a statement that the bundle is limited or incomplete. The summary should be limited to those matters which the court needs to know for the purpose of the hearing and for management of the case.

2.3 The requirement to provide a bundle shall not apply to the hearing of any urgent application where the circumstances are such that it is not reasonably practicable for a bundle to be provided.

3.1 At the commencement of the bundle there shall be:

(a) A summary of the background to the hearing limited, if practicable, to one A4 page;

(b) A statement of the issue or issues to be determined;

(c) A summary of the order or directions sought by each party;

(d) A chronology if it is a final hearing or if the summary under (a) is insufficient;

(e) Skeleton arguments as may be appropriate, with copies of all authorities relied on.

3.2 If possible the bundle shall be agreed. In all cases, the party preparing the bundle shall paginate it and provide an index to all other parties prior to the hearing.

3.3 The bundle should normally be contained in a ring binder or lever arch file (limited to 350 pages in each file). Where there is more than one bundle, each should be clearly distinguishable. Bundles shall be lodged, if practicable, 2 clear days prior to the hearing. For hearings in the Royal Courts of Justice bundles shall be lodged with the Clerk of the Rules. All bundles shall have clearly marked on the outside, the title and number of the case, the hearing date and time and, if known, the name of the Judge hearing the case.

4. After each hearing which is not a final hearing, the party responsible for the bundle shall retrieve it from the court. The bundle with any additional documents shall be re-lodged for further hearings in accordance with the above provisions.

5. This direction replaces paragraphs 5 and 8 of the direction "Case Management" dated 31st January 1995 and shall have effect from the 2nd May 2000.

6. Issued with the approval and concurrence of the Lord Chancellor.

A(e) Timetable

- File Form A. Court to serve copy on the Respondent within 4 days (r. 2.61A(4)(b)).

- Applicant to serve mortgagees and pension fund trustees/managers (r. 2.59(4) and r. 2.70(4)).

- Not later than 35 days before the First Appointment, both parties simultaneously to exchange Form Es (r. 2.61B(2)).

- Applicant to serve trustees, settlors and disponees (r. 2.59(3)).

- At least 14 days before the First Appointment, both parties to file and serve (r. 2.61B(7) to (9)):

  (a) a concise statement of the issues;

  (b) a chronology;

  (c) a questionnaire;

  (d) Form G (see precedent B2(h)); and

  (e) (applicant only) confirmation of service on mortgagees, trustees, settlors, disponees and pension fund trustees/managers.

- Both parties to prepare written costs estimates for the First Appointment (r. 2.61F(1)).

- **The First Appointment**   The District Judge to:

  (a) give directions as to questionnaires, valuations etc. (r. 2.61D(2)(a) and (b)); and

  (b) fix the Financial Dispute Resolution appointment or further directions appointment etc. (r. 2.61D(2)(c) and (d)).

- Not later than 7 days before the Financial Dispute Resolution appointment, the applicant to file copies of offers and responses, whether open, without prejudice or *Calderbank* (r. 2.61E(3)).

- Both parties to prepare written costs estimates for the Financial Dispute Resolution Appointment (r. 2.61F(1)).

- **Financial Dispute Resolution appointment** (a without prejudice appointment—see *Practice Direction*, set out in A(g) at pp. 48–49) The judge, in the absence of settlement, to give further directions, including, where appropriate, fixing a final hearing date (r. 2.61E(8)) and directing narrative affidavits (*W v. W (Ancillary Relief: Practice)* [2000] Fam. Law 473).

- Not later than 14 days before the final hearing, the applicant to file and serve an open statement setting out concise details, including the amounts involved, of the orders proposed by him (r. 2.69E(1)).

- Not more than 7 days thereafter, the respondent to file a similar open statement (r. 2.69E(2)).

- Both parties to prepare written costs estimates for the final hearing (r. 2.61F(1)).

- **The final hearing**

A(f) Statement of Costs (Form 1, CPR Part 48)

Court   Case reference   **A90**
Judge/Master
Case title

               [*Party*'s Statement of Costs for the hearing on [*date*]

Description of fee earners
    (1) [*name*] [*grade*] [*hourly rate claimed*]
    (2) [*name*] [*grade*] [*hourly rate claimed*]

Attendances on [*Party*]
    [*number*] hours at £   £

Attendances on opponents
    [*number*] hours at £   £

Attendances on others
    (1) [*number*] hours at £   £
    (2) [*number*] hours at £   £

Site inspection etc.
    [*number*] hours at £   £

Work done on negotiations
    [*number*] hours at £   £

Other work not covered above
    [*number*] hours at £   £

Work done on documents
    [*number*] hours at £   £

Attendance at hearing
    [*number*] hours at £   £
    [*number*] hours travel and waiting at £   £

Counsel's fees [*name*] [*year of call*]
    Fee for [*advice/conference/documents*]   £

Fee for hearing   £

Other expenses
    [court fees]   £
    Others *[give brief description]*   £_____

TOTAL
    Amount of VAT claimed: £
        on solicitor's and counsel's fees   £
        on other expenses   £_____

GRAND TOTAL   £_____

The costs estimated above do not exceed the costs which the *[party]* is liable to pay in respect of the work which this estimate covers.

Dated   Signed
              Name of firm of solicitors
              [partner] for the *[party]*

[Three grades of fee-earner are suggested:

    (a)   solicitors with over four years' post-qualification experience;

    (b)   other solicitors and legal executives and fee-earners of equivalent experience;

    (c)   trainee solicitors and fee-earners of equivalent experience;

"Legal executive" means a Fellow of the Institute of Legal Executives. Those who are not Fellows of the Institute are not entitled to call themselves legal executives and in principle therefore not entitled to the same hourly rate as a legal executive. In respect of each fee-earner, communications should be treated as attendances and routine communications should be claimed at one-tenth of the hourly rate.]

47

A(g) Practice Direction (Pre-application protocol)

Ancillary relief procedure—Pre-application protocol—Financial dispute resolution appointment

---

(1) Introduction

(1.1) The Family Proceedings (Amendment No 2) Rules 1999 (SI 1999/3491) make important amendments to the Family Proceedings Rules 1991 (SI 1991/1247) ("FPR 1991"), as from 5 June 2000. The existing "pilot scheme" rules in relation to ancillary relief which have applied since 1996 but only in specified courts will become, with significant revisions, of general application. In the same way as the pilot scheme, the new procedure is intended to reduce delay, facilitate settlements, limit costs incured by parties and provide the court with greater and more effective control over the conduct of the proceedings.

(2) Pre-application protocol

(2.1) The "Pre-application protocol" annexed to this Direction outlines the steps parties should take to seek and provide information from and to each other prior to the commencement of any ancillary relief application. The court will expect the parties to comply with the terms of the protocol.

(3) Financial dispute resolution ("FDR") appointment

(3.1) A key element in the new procedure is the Financial Dispute Resolution ("FDR") appointment. Rule 2.61E provides that the FDR appointment is to be treated as a meeting held for the purposes of discussion and negotiation. Such meetings which were previously described as meetings held for the purposes of conciliation have been developed as a means of reducing the tension which inevitably arises in matrimonial and family disputes and facilitating settlement of those disputes.

(3.2) In order for the FDR appointment to be effective, parties must approach the occasion openly and without reserve. Non-disclosure of the content of such meetings is accordingly vital and is an essential prerequisite for fruitful discussion directed to the settlement of the dispute between the parties. The FDR appointment is an important part of the settlement process. As a consequence of *Re D (Minors) (Conciliation. Disclosure of information)* [1993] Fam 231, sub nom *Re D (Minors) (Conciliation: Privilege)* [1993] 1 FLR 932, evidence of anything said or of any admission made in the course of an FDR appointment will not be admissible in evidence, except at the trial of a person for an offence committed at the appointment or in the very exceptional circumstances indicated in *Re D*.

(3.3) Courts will therefore expect:

- parties to make offers and proposals;

- recipients of offers and proposals to give them proper consideration;

- that parties, whether separately or together, will not seek to exclude from consideration at the appointment any such offer or proposal.

(3.4) In order to make the most effective use of the first appointment and the FDR appointment, the legal representatives attending those appointments will be expected to have full knowledge of the case.

(4) Single joint expert

(4.1) The introduction of expert evidence in proceedings is likely to increase costs substantially and consequently the court will use its powers to restrict the unnecessary use of experts. Accordingly, where expert evidence is sought to be relied upon, parties should if possible agree upon a single expert whom they can jointly instruct. Where parties are unable to agree upon the expert to be instructed, the court will consider using its powers under Part 35 of the Civil Procedure Rules 1998 (SI 1998/3132) to direct that evidence be given by one expert only. In such cases parties must be in a position at the first appointment or when the matter comes to be considered by the court to provide the court with a list of suitable experts or to make submissions as to the method by which the expert is to be selected.

(5) This Direction shall have effect as from 5 June 2000 and replaces *Practice Direction: Ancillary Relief Procedure: Pilot Scheme* (16 June 1997) [1997] 2 FLR 304.

(6) Issued with the approval and concurrence of the Lord Chancellor.

25 May 2000   DAME ELIZABETH BUTLER-SLOSS
                                            President

Pre-application protocol

1. Introduction

1.1.

    1.1.1. Lord Woolf in his final Access to Justice Report of July 1996 recommended the development of pre-action protocols:

        "to build on and increase the benefits of early but well informed settlement which genuinely satisfy both parties to dispute"

    1.1.2. Subsequently, in April 2000, the Lord Chancellor's Ancillary Relief Advisory Group agreed this pre-application protocol.

1.2. The aim of the pre-action protocol is to ensure that:

    (a) Pre-application disclosure and negotiation takes place in appropriate cases.

    (b) Where there is pre-application disclosure and negotiation, it is dealt with:
        i. Cost effectively;
        ii. In line with the overriding objective of the Family Proceedings (Amendments) Rules 1999;

    (c) The parties are in a position to settle the case fairly and early without litigation.

1.3. The court will be able to treat the standard set in the pre-application protocol as the normal reasonable approach to pre-application conduct. If proceedings are subsequently issued, the court will be entitled to decide whether there has been non-compliance with the protocol and, if so, whether non-compliance merits consequences.

2. Notes of Guidance

Scope of the Protocol   A100

2.1. This protocol is intended to apply to all claims for ancillary relief as defined by FPR r. 1(2). It is designed to cover all classes of case, ranging from a simple application for periodical payments to an application for a substantial lump sum and property adjustment order, The protocol is designed to facilitate the operation of what was called the pilot scheme and is from June 5, 2000 the standard procedure for ancillary relief applications.

2.2. In considering the option of pre-application disclosure and negotiation, solicitors should bear in mind the advantage of having a court timetable and court managed process. There is sometimes an advantage in preparing disclosure before proceedings are commenced. However, solicitors should bear in mind the objective of controlling costs and in particular the costs of discovery and that the option of pre-application disclosure and negotiation has risks of excessive and uncontrolled expenditure and delay. This option should only be encouraged where both parties agree to follow this route and disclosure is not likely to be an issue or has been adequately dealt with in mediation or otherwise.

2.3. Solicitors should consider at an early stage and keep under review whether it would be appropriate to suggest mediation to the clients as an alternative to solicitor negotiation or court based litigation.

2.4. Making an application to the court should not be regarded as a hostile step or a last resort, rather as a way of starting the court timetable, controlling disclosure and endeavouring to avoid the costly final hearing and the preparation for it.

First Letter   A101

2.5 The circumstances of parties to an application for ancillary relief are so various that it would be difficult to prepare a specimen letter of claim. The request for information will be different in every case. However, the tone of the initial letter is important and the guidelines in para 3.7 should be followed. It should be approved in advance by the client. Solicitors writing to an unrepresented party should always recommend that he seeks independent legal advice and enclose a second copy of the letter to be passed to any solicitor instructed. A reasonable time limit for a response may be 14 days.

Negotiation and Settlement   A102

2.6. In the event of pre-application disclosure and negotiation, as envisaged in paragraph 2.2, an application should not be issued when a settlement is a reasonable prospect.

Disclosure   A103

2.7. The protocol underlines the obligation of parties to make full and frank disclosure of all material facts, documents and other information relevant to the issues. Solicitors owe their clients a duty to tell them in clear terms of this duty and of the possible consequences of breach of the duty. This duty of disclosure is an ongoing obligation and includes the duty to disclose any material changes after initial disclosure has been given. Solicitors are referred to the Good Practice Guide for Disclosure produced by the Solicitors Family Law Association (obtainable from the Administrative Director, 366A Crofton Road, Orpington, Kent BR2 8NN).

3. The Protocol

General Principles   A104

3.1. All parties must always bear in mind the overriding objective set out at FPR Rule 2.51B and try to ensure that all claims should be resolved and a just resolution achieved as speedily as possible without costs being unreasonably incurred. The needs of any children should be addressed and safeguarded. The procedures which it is appropriate to follow should be conducted with minimum distress to the parties and in a manner designed to promote as good a continuing relationship between the parties and any children affected as is possible in the circumstances.

3.2. The principle of proportionality must be borne in mind at all times. It is unacceptable for the costs of any case to be disproportionate to the financial value of the subject matter of the dispute.

3.3. Parties should be informed that, where a Court exercises a discretion as to whether costs are payable by one party to another, this discretion extends to pre-application offers to settle and conduct of disclosure (rule 44.3 paragraph 1 of the Civil Procedure Rules 1998).

Identifying the Issues   A105

3.4. Parties must seek to clarify their claims and identify the issues between them as soon as possible. So that this can be achieved they must provide full, frank and clear disclosure of facts, information and documents which are material and sufficiently accurate to enable proper negotiations to take place to settle their differences. Openness in all dealings is essential.

Disclosure   A106

3.5. If parties carry out voluntary disclosure before the issue of proceedings, the parties should exchange schedules of assets, income, liabilities and other material facts, using Form E as a guide to the format of the disclosure. Documents should only be disclosed to the extent that they are required by Form E. Excessive or disproportionate costs should not be incurred.

Correspondence A107

3.6. Any first letter and subsequent correspondence must focus on the clarification of claims and identification of issues and their resolution. Protracted and unnecessary correspondence and 'trial by correspondence' must be avoided.

3.7 The impact of any correspondence upon the reader and in particular the parties must always be considered. Any correspondence which raises irrelevant issues or which might cause the other party to adopt an entrenched, polarised or hostile position is to be discouraged.

3.8. Expert valuation evidence is only necessary where the parties cannot agree or do not know the value of some significant asset. The cost of a valuation should be proportionate to the sums in dispute. Wherever possible, valuations of properties, shares etc should be obtained from a single valuer instructed by both parties. To that end, a party wishing to instruct an expert (the first party) should first give the other party a list of the names of one or more experts in the relevant speciality whom he considers are suitable to instruct. Within 14 days the other party may indicate an objection to one or more of the named experts and, if so, should supply the names of one or more experts whom he considers suitable.

3.9. Where the identity of the expert is agreed, the parties should agree the terms of a joint letter of instructions.

3.10 Where no agreement is reached as to the identity of the expert, each party should think carefully before instructing his own expert because of the costs implications. Disagreements about disclosure such as the use and identity of an expert may be better managed by the court within the context of an application for ancillary relief.

3.11. Whether a joint report is commissioned or the parties have chosen to instruct separate experts, it is important that the expert is prepared to answer reasonable questions raised by either party.

3.12. When experts' reports are commissioned pre-application, it should be made clear to the experts that they may in due course be reporting to the court and that they should therefore consider themselves bound by the guidance as to expert witnesses in Part 39 of the Civil Procedure Rules 1998.

3.13 Where the parties propose to instruct a joint expert, there is a duty on both parties to disclose whether they have already consulted that expert about the assets in issue.

3.14. If the parties agree to instruct separate experts the parties should be encouraged to agree in advance that the reports will be disclosed.

Summary A108

3.15. The aim of all pre-application proceedings steps must be to assist the parties to resolve their differences speedily and fairly or at least narrow the issues and, should that not be possible, to assist the court to do so.

A(h) Estimate of Costs (Form H)

A110

Ancillary Relief

Costs Estimate of

*[Applicant]

*[Respondent]

In the	
*[County Court] ***[Principal Registry of the Family Division]**	
Case No. *Always quote this*	
Applicant's Solicitor's reference	
Respondent's Solicitor's reference	

(*delete as appropriate)

The marriage of   and

PART 1

	Legal Aid Rates £	Indemnity Rate £
1. Ancillary relief solicitor's costs *(including VAT)* including costs of the current hearing, and any previous solicitor's costs.		
2. Disbursements *(include VAT, if appropriate, and any incurred by previous solicitors)*		
3. All Counsel's fees *(including VAT)*		
TOTAL		

PART 2

4. Add any private cases costs previously incurred *(Legal Aid cases only)*		
5. GRAND TOTAL		

PART 3

6. State what has been paid towards the total at 5 above		
7. Amount of any contributions paid by the assisted person towards their legal aid certificate		

NB. If you are Legally Aided and might be seeking an order for costs against the other party complete both rates.

Dated

The court office at

is open between 10 am and 4 pm (4.30pm at the Principal Registry of the Family Division) Monday to Friday. When corresponding with the court, please address forms or letters to the Court Manager and quote the case number. If you do not do so, your correspondence may be returned.

Form H Costs Estimate

A(i) Statement of information (Form M1)

Statement of information on application for consent order (printed form)

In the	County Court		**A120**
	No of matter		
Between	Petitioner	*Solicitor's ref*	
and	Respondent	*Solicitor's ref*	

Statement of information for a consent order

Duration of Marriage

Give the date of your marriage and the date of the decree absolute (if pronounced)

Age of parties

Give the age of any minor (ie under the age of 18) or dependent child(ren) of the family.

Summary of means

Give, as at the date this statement is signed overleaf:

(1) the approximate amount or value of **capital resources**. *If there is a property give its net equity and details of the proposed distribution of the equity.*

(2) the **net income** *of the petitioner and respondent and, where relevant, of minor or dependent child(ren) of the family.*

(3) the value of any benefits under a **pension scheme** *which you have or are likely to have, including the most recent valuation (if any) provided by the pension scheme.*

Note: if the application is only made for an order for interim periodical payments, or for variation of an order for periodical payments, you only need to give details of 'net income'.

Where the parties and the children will live

Give details of the arrangements which are intended for the accommodation of each of the parties and any minor or dependent child(ren) of the family.

	(1) Capital Resources (less any unpaid mortgage or charge)	(2) Net income	(3) Pension
Petitioner			
Respondent			
Children			

Petitioner   Respondent

Child(ren)

Marital plans

Please tick a box and, if appropriate, give the date of the marriage if you know it.

	No intention to marry or cohabit at present	Has remarried	Intends to marry	Intends to cohabit with another person
Petitioner	☐	☐ Date of marriage:	☐ Date of marriage:	☐
Respondent	☐	☐ Date of marriage:	☐ Date of marriage:	☐

Notice to Mortgagee

These questions are to be answered by the applicant where the terms of the order provide for a transfer of property.

Has every mortgagee (if any) of the property been served with notice of the application? Yes ☐ No ☐

Has any objection to a transfer of property been made by any mortgagee, within 14 days from the date when the notice of the application was served? Yes ☐ No ☐

Notice to Pension Fund or Insurance Scheme

These questions are to be answered by the applicant where the terms of an order under section 23 of the Matrimonial Causes Act 1973 include provision by virtue of section 25B and section 25C of that Act.

Has every Trustee or Manager of any pension fund, insurance scheme or similar arrangement been served with notice of the application and notice under Rule 2.70(4)(a)(b) and (c) of the Family Proceedings Rules 1991? Yes ☐ No ☐

Has any objection to an order under section 23 of the Matrimonial Causes Act 1973 which includes provision by virtue of section 25B and section 25C of that Act been made by a Trustee or Manager within 14 days from the date when the notice of the application was served? Yes ☐ No ☐

Other information

Gives details of any other especially significant matters.

Signed

[Solicitor for] Petitioner | [Solicitor for] Respondent

Date | Date

B   Evidence

B(a) Specimen questions

Bank and building society accounts **B2**

1. A schedule of all (current, deposit, loan or other) bank accounts which the Respondent has held in his sole name, jointly with any other person(s) or by his nominee(s), or in which he has had any beneficial interest, whether in the United Kingdom or anywhere else in the world, during the last [1 *or* 3] years [*or* since _____ 19_____].

2. A schedule of all building society or other savings or deposit accounts (not covered by paragraph 1 above) which the Respondent has held in his sole name, jointly with any other person(s) or by his nominee(s), or in which he has had any beneficial interest, whether in the United Kingdom or anywhere else in the world, during the last [1 *or* 3] years [*or* since _____ 19____].

3. Copy statements/pass books relating to all accounts referred to in paragraphs 1 and 2 above in respect of the period from _____ 19 ____ to the date of answering this questionnaire, and continuing thereafter to the date of trial unless the Petitioner's Solicitors give notice to the contrary.

4. Identification of (a) all credit entries appearing in the said statements/pass books of [£100] or more and (b) all debit entries of [£500] or more.

[Note: such a request should not be regarded as automatic. It is true that bank etc. statements are usually uninformative without explanation of the principal entries, but it is often more appropriate to peruse the statements provided before any decision is made as to whether identification of certain entries is required and, if so, whether a threshold, such as in the example, would be appropriate.

It is the usual practice of the Principal Registry to refuse at the First Appointment any requests for statements going back much beyond one year. It is felt that in most cases this will give sufficient disclosure for the Financial Dispute Resolution appointment. If appropriate, an application can be renewed later.]

5. As to the statements already produced by the Respondent, please identify the following credit and debit entries:

Bankers, correspondence with   B3

Copies of all correspondence passing between the Respondent [or his accountants] on the one hand and his bankers (or any of them) on the other hand during the last [3] years. Alternatively, if such correspondence is voluminous, please confirm that it will be made available for inspection by the Petitioner's Solicitors on request.

Chattels   B4

As to the furniture and other contents of the former matrimonial home:

(a) A copy of the household insurance policy under which they are insured, together with copies of any schedules thereto.

(b) Has any inventory or valuation, whether in connection with such insurance or otherwise, been taken or made during the last five years? If so, a copy is requested.

Cohabitee: dispositions to B5

Has the Respondent made any financial dispositions, in cash or in kind, to the Co–Respondent? If so, please give full particulars, disclosing any documents relating thereto in the custody, possession or power of the Respondent and identifying any relevant entry in the Respondent's bank or building society statements/passbooks.

Cohabitee: means of B6

To the best of the knowledge, information and belief of the [Respondent], what are the means and other relevant circumstances of [the Co-Respondent]?

[Note: if a party contends that he has attempted unsuccessfully to obtain these details, consideration can be given to applying for an inspection appointment under Family Proceedings Rules 1991, r. 2.62(7) or to serving a witness summons or subpoena.]

Company (private): accounts and other information B7

As to the company _____ Limited ("the company"):

(a) Copies of the Accounts of the company (if necessary in draft) for the years ended _____.

(b) If the Accounts of the company for the year ended _____ 20 _____ are not yet available, even in draft, when is it expected that their preparation will be completed? A letter from the company's accountants explaining the position is requested.

(c) Copies of any existing management accounts in respect of the period from the date of the last accounts provided in answer to (a) above to the date of answering this questionnaire.

(d) Does the Respondent consider that any of the assets and liabilities of the company have a value different from that shown in the Balance Sheet? If so, please provide details.

(e) As to the Accounts of the company for the year ended _____ 20 _____ already disclosed by the Respondent:

[for example]

[(i) Identify the land and buildings appearing under Note 1 (Fixed Assets) at a cost value of £26,565.

(ii) Have there been any, and, if so, what, professional valuations of the land and buildings in question during the last three years? If so, please produce copies. In any event, what is the Respondent's estimate of their current open market value?

(iii) Explain precisely the entry "Management charges £25,500" which appears in the Trading Profit and Loss Account.]

(f) Please confirm that, upon reasonable notice, the accountants instructed on behalf of the Petitioner in connection with these proceedings will be granted the facility to inspect the company's books and other documentary records.

[*Note: this is a good example of a request which in normal circumstances would be regarded as oppressive and unnecessary, a fortiori if the accounts of the company in question have been audited. The court can be expected to set its face against an inquiry which amounts to nothing more than a fishing expedition and, if such a request were to be opposed, the subsequent application for specific discovery would in practice have to be supported by an affidavit from the Petitioner's accountant justifying the depth of the proposed investigation.*]

(g) Copies of the Memorandum and Articles of Association of the company.

(h) What is the Respondent's case as to the value properly to be attributed to his shareholding in the company? A reasoned valuation by the company's accountants or accountants appointed on the Respondent's behalf in connection with these proceedings is requested, together with copies of any documentation (including but not limited to any valuation by or correspondence with the Share Valuation Division of the Inland Revenue) which has come into existence during the last three years and which is relevant to the value of the shares in the company (for whatever purpose) during that period.

[*Note: whether this request is appropriate depends upon the facts of the particular case. N.B. the warning given by the Court of Appeal in Potter v. Potter [1982] 1 W.L.R. 1255. See also B v. B (Financial Provision) [1989] 1 F.L.R. 119.*]

Company (private): prospects of flotation or takeover   B8

Have any, and, if so, what, plans been canvassed between the Respondent and/or his fellow–directors of the company and/or the company's professional advisers as to the possibility of the company being publicly floated, whether on the Unlisted Securities Market or otherwise? If so, copies of all documents relating thereto in the custody, possession or power of the Respondent are requested, including but not limited to all minutes and memorandums of any board or other meetings in which the possibility of such flotation has been discussed. [Please confirm in any event that the company's Minute Book will be made available for inspection on request.]

Has the company (or the Respondent or other representative or agent personally) received any offers, approaches or overtures for its acquisition in whole or in part by any person or by another corporate entity as a going concern? If so, full particulars are requested, together with all documents relating thereto in the custody, possession or power of the Respondent, including but not limited to all minutes and memorandums of any board or other meetings in which the possibility of such acquisition has been discussed. [Please confirm in any event that the company's Minute Book will be made available for inspection on request.]

Company (private): directorships generally   B9

Give full particulars of all company directorships held by the Respondent during the last [3] years.

Without prejudice to the generality of the foregoing, has the Respondent ever been a director of or had any, and, if so, what, connection with a company called _____ or bearing some similar name?

Company (private): position of the spouse asking the questions   B10

1. In the Accounts for the year ended _____ exactly what remuneration, National Insurance contributions, pension contributions, benefits and other payments to, for, or in respect of the Petitioner were paid? Please identify within which figures in the Accounts they are included.

2. Please produce a letter from the company's accountants showing all outstanding and potential future liabilities to tax, National Insurance or other similar charges in relation to her involvement with the company and the possible transfer of her shareholding in the company.

3. Does the Petitioner have any outstanding or potential liabilities to or in relation to the company? If so, please provide full details.

4. Without prejudice to the generality of the immediately foregoing question, please obtain a letter from the company's bankers specifying exactly what liabilities and potential liabilities she has to them under any guarantee, mortgage, charge or other similar arrangement and produce copies of the relevant documents.

5. Has the Respondent made any enquiries of the company's bankers about releasing the Petitioner from liability to them? If so, please provide full details. If not, please make the appropriate enquiries and make the results known to the Petitioner's solicitors. [In particular and without prejudice to the generality of the

foregoing, please obtain a letter from the _____ Bank plc confirming on what terms they are prepared to release the second charge on the former matrimonial home.]

Credit cards   B11

Of what credit [, account or charge] cards, whether or not in his own name, has the Respondent had the use during the last [3] years? Please produce the statements relating to all such cards to cover the period from [*e.g. date 12 months earlier*] _____ 20 _____ to the date of answering this questionnaire (and continuing to the date of trial, unless the Petitioner's solicitors give notice to the contrary). In the event that any of the items of expenditure appearing on the said statements were reimbursed by the Respondent's employers, please mark the statements accordingly.

Director's loan account   B12

A copy of the company's private ledger or other documentary record of all movements which have taken place on the Respondent's director's loan or current account between _____ 20 _____ and the date of answering this questionnaire (and continuing thereafter until the date of trial, unless the Petitioner's Solicitors give notice to the contrary).

Please explain the source and destination of all credit and debit entries respectively which appear in the said ledger or record, insofar as they are not apparent from it.

Earning capacity   B13

What is the Respondent's case as to her earning capacity? In particular:

[*for example*]

(a) Is it accepted that, having regard to her obligations to the children of the family, the Respondent is now able to take full-time employment? If not, please give the reasons.

(b) Does the Respondent contend that, in order to exploit her secretarial skills, she needs to take some form of refresher course (which, for the avoidance of doubt, the Petitioner is prepared to finance)?

(c) Is it disputed that, as a full-time secretary, the Petitioner could earn approximately £20,000 gross per annum in the area of the former matrimonial home?

Employment, attempts to obtain   B14

What attempts has the Respondent made to obtain employment since _____ 20 _____ ? A full narrative account is requested, accompanied by copies of all relevant documents, including advertisements answered, job applications and responses from prospective employers.

Has the Respondent registered with any, and if so, which, employment agencies and on what dates?

Holidays, travel abroad generally   B15

Copies of all [save the blank] pages of the Respondent's passport(s), to cover the period from the _____ 20 _____ to the date of answering this questionnaire.

A schedule of all trips abroad made by the Respondent during this period, stating in respect of each trip:

(a) whether the same was a holiday or in connection with business or both;

(b) by whom the Respondent was accompanied;

(c) the expenditure incurred by the Respondent; and

(d) the source of the funds so expended.

Income: rental   B16

As to the rental income received by the Respondent in respect of _____:

(a) accounts of all such income and the expenditure referable thereto for the last [2] years;

(b) copies of all tenancy agreements in respect of the same period.

Income: company director   B17

A schedule of all director's remuneration, including salary, fees and bonuses received by the Respondent during the last three years.

Does the Respondent have any expectation of an increase in his remuneration in the foreseeable future? If so, please give full particulars.

Copies of the three Forms P11D most recently submitted to the Inland Revenue, together with the accompanying claims under section 198 of the Income and Corporation Taxes Act 1988.

Please specify all fringe benefits directly or indirectly enjoyable by the Respondent arising out of his employment by the company, and state precisely to what extent they are taxed as such by the Inland Revenue.

A copy of the Respondent's service contract and copies of all correspondence passing between the Respondent and his present employers which contains reference to the terms upon which he is employed.

Income: partnership   B18

As to the partnership _____, please produce:

(a) a copy of the partnership deed;

(b) the Accounts of the partnership in respect of the last 3 available years. In the event that the Accounts for the year to _____ 20 _____ have not yet been completed, please state when their completion is expected and meanwhile produce all management accounts or their equivalent.

[*Note: a complaint that disclosure of partnership accounts will infringe the privacy of other partners is often made. A standard compromise is the provision of copies of the accounts with appropriate deletions.*]

Income: salaried employee   B19

Copies of the Respondent's Forms P60 in respect of the years to 5th April 19 _____, 19 _____ and 19 _____.

From and including the month of April 19 _____, copies of all the Respondent's payslips.

When does the Respondent expect his next salary review, and has he received any, and, if so, what, indication of the increase in salary that can reasonably be anticipated?

Income: self-employed   B20

Copies of the Accounts of the Respondent for the years ended _____ 19 _____, 19 _____ and 19 _____.

As to the Accounts already produced in respect of the year to _____
19 ____, please give a precise breakdown of the following items of expenditure,
namely: _____.

Income: tax returns and assessments   B21

Copies of the Respondent's Tax Returns and Assessments, with all supporting
schedules referred to therein, in respect of the years of assessment 1996/7, 1997/8
and 1998/9.

Insurance (life policies)   B22

Please produce a schedule of all life insurance policies on the Respondent's life
and/or of which he is an actual or potential beneficiary and/or in respect of which
he pays or has paid the premiums, giving in the case of each policy [a letter from
the relevant company setting out] the following particulars:

 (a) Insurance company;

 (b) Policy number;

 (c) Type of policy;

 (d) Sum assured;

 (e) Premiums payable;

 (f) Maturity date;

 (g) Surrender value (if applicable);

 (h) The projected sum, inclusive of bonuses, payable upon maturity (if appli-
      cable) [the letter from the company specifically to say whether all potential
      terminal bonuses are included];

 (i) Any trusts, assignments, loans or notices affecting the policy.

Investments: Business Expansion Scheme   B23

Any reports or memorandums, whether compiled by the relevant fund man-
ager(s) or otherwise, which refer or are relevant to the actual or potential value of
the Respondent's investments under the Business Expansion Scheme.

Investments: stocks and shares, unit trusts etc.   B24

If and insofar as this information is not apparent from the Respondent's Tax Returns, a schedule, with dates, of all dealings in stocks, shares, unit trusts and other publicly quoted investments made by the Respondent since 6th April 20 ____. In the case of any such investment which has either cost or yielded proceeds of sale of or in excess of £_____, identify the source and destination of the acquisition cost and proceeds of sale respectively.

An updated summary prepared by the Respondent's stock-brokers of his portfolio of investments (to include the base cost in respect of each investment and its yield).

What, according to the Respondent's accountants, would be the Respondent's liability for Capital Gains Tax if his entire portfolio of investments were disposed of, and how is it calculated?

Jewellery   B25

Has there been any valuation of the Respondent's jewellery since _____ 20 ____. If so, please produce a copy. If not, please confirm that the Respondent's jewellery will be made available for an inspection and valuation on request.

Land: acquisition or disposal, particulars of   B26

In respect of the purchase of _____ please provide or explain:

(a) Copy completion statement relating to the acquisition of the property;

(b) Copy mortgage deed;

(c) Copy of the mortgage application submitted to the mortgagee including any personal information form and any other documents submitted by or on behalf of the Respondent;

(d) The amount and the source of the deposit; and

(e) The amount and the source of the funds spent upon the renovations and improvements to the property.

In respect of the sale of _____ please provide or explain:

(a) Copy completion statement relating to the sale of the property; and

(b) The precise destination of the net proceeds of sale, with cross–reference to the relevant credit entries in the Respondent's bank and building society statements and pass books.

Land: mortgaged to bank   B27

In respect of the mortgage over _____ in favour of _____, please provide:

(a) A copy of the mortgage deed;

(b) A letter from the mortgagee specifying the amount or amounts currently secured by the mortgage, with reference to each and every account (whether presently in credit or debit and whether or not in his own name) which is or may potentially be covered by the security.

Land: office copy entries   B28

Please provide copies of up-to-date office copy entries in relation to the property at _____ [including the land adjacent thereto owned by the Respondent].

[*Note: these may now be obtained direct from the Land Registry by any member of the public.*]

Land: unregistered   B29

Please provide a copy of the conveyance or conveyances to the Respondent of the property known as _____, together with an abstract of title or other documents showing the rights and incumbrances to which the land is subject or of which it has the benefit.

Land: value, request for estimate   B30

How much does the Respondent estimate that the property known as _____, is worth, and upon what information and other considerations is the estimate based? In the event that the property has in fact been professionally valued during the course of the last 3 years, please produce copies of such valuation(s).

Land: alternative request for information on valuations B31

Has the Respondent at any time since _____ 19____ had any valuation or estimate, whether formal or informal, written or otherwise, of the value of _____? If so, please provide full details.

Lloyd's B32

As to the Respondent's membership of Lloyd's:

(a) What has been his premium income limit from and including the Lloyd's year of account 19 ____?

(b) The Petitioner reserves her position as to disclosure of detailed syndicate accounts and other documents, but in the first instance the Respondent is requested to produce all Personal Account Summaries or their equivalent submitted to him in respect of the Lloyd's years of account 19 ____, 19 ____ and 19 ____, and also a letter or memorandum from his underwriting agents in which they give a full breakdown of the said figures by reference inter alia to

  (i) underwriting profits and losses;
  (ii) syndicate investment income;
  (iii) capital appreciation; and
  (iv) in each case, the fiscal treatment thereof.

(c) Please produce documentary evidence of the present investments held by the Respondent or on his behalf in Lloyd's Deposit, Special Reserve and Personal Reserve.

Loans: made by respondent B33

As to the loan of £_____ allegedly made by the Respondent to _____ [and said to have been written off by him]:

(a) What was the precise date of the loan?

(b) What was the source of the monies advanced? Documentary evidence (if possible, the cancelled cheque) is requested.

(c) Precisely what representations were made by _____ as to the purpose for which the loan was required and [her] intentions as to repayment?

(d) What were the terms of repayment, and were they oral or in writing? If the latter, produce copies of all relevant documents.

71

(e) Does the Respondent concede that the loan was made without the Petitioner's knowledge or approval?

Loans: made to respondent   B34

As to the loan of £_____ allegedly made by _____ in 20 _____:

(a) What was the precise date of the loan?

(b) Was it made by cheque and, if not, by what other method of payment?

(c) Produce the relevant statement of the bank account into which the said monies were (presumably) paid by the Respondent.

(d) What were the precise terms of the loan, as to repayment and generally?

(e) Produce copies of all other documents relating to the loan which are in the custody, possession or power of the Respondent.

Pension arrangements   B35

As to the Respondent's employers' pension scheme, please produce:

(a) A copy both of the rules of the scheme and of any explanatory booklet available to its members;

(b) A letter or memorandum from the secretary to the trustees of the scheme or some other suitable source explaining and quantifying the projected benefits which either the Petitioner or the Respondent may be expected (or, but for the dissolution of the marriage, might have been expected) to enjoy under the scheme. Without prejudice to the generality of the foregoing, particulars are requested of the amount of:

   (i) the lump sum payable in the event of the Respondent's death in service;
  (ii) the widow's pension payable in the event of the Respondent's death in service;
 (iii) the Respondent's pension which will be receivable upon his retirement in the event of his not commuting any part thereof for a lump sum;
 (iv) the maximum lump sum which the Respondent could receive in part commutation of his pension; and
  (v) the Respondent's pension in the event of such commutation;

   [For the avoidance of doubt, the figures requested under sub–paragraphs (iii), (iv) and (v) should be calculated on the basis of the Respondent's estimated salary at retirement.]

(c) In the event that the lump sum payable upon the Respondent's death in service falls to be distributed at the trustee's discretion, has the Respondent made any nomination or expression of wish as to the person or persons to whom he would like the said sum distributed? If so, please produce a copy of the relevant document(s).

(d) In the event that it is not clear from the answers to the foregoing questions, please state whether the Respondent is entitled to surrender a portion of the scheme for the benefit of his spouse.

Pension: completion of question 2.16 in Form E   B36

Please obtain from [all the companies with which the Respondent has pension policies] the attached form [*i.e. the relevant page from Form E*] duly completed.

Pre-nuptial agreement   B37

As to the pre-nuptial agreement between the parties:

(a) please produce a copy;

(b) confirm that the Respondent had received legal advice before signing it.

[*Such agreements, whilst not binding, may be a section 25 consideration (see N v. N (Foreign Divorce: Financial Relief) [1997] 1 F.L.R. 900 and S v. S (Divorce: Staying Proceedings) [1997] 2 F.L.R. 100). A party is not entitled to require the other party to disclose the nature of the advice received (Stephenson v. Stephenson (1997) unreported, 9 May, CA).*]

Remarriage or cohabitation, intention of   B38

Does the Respondent have any and, if so, what intention of remarriage to or cohabitation with another [man]? Without prejudice to the generality of this question, please state with appropriate narrative the precise nature of the Respondent's relationship with [the Co-Respondent], giving full particulars of any direct or indirect financial support that the Respondent has received from [the Co-Respondent] since the beginning of their relationship or expects to receive hereafter.

Safe deposit box   B39

Has the Respondent had the use of any safe deposit box during the last [2] years? If so:

(a) At what bank(s) or other financial institution(s)?

73

(b) Please provide a detailed schedule of the present contents of each such box.

(c) Please provide full particulars of all items removed from each such box during the last 12 months.

[Note: many banks and financial institutions keep a documentary record of the date and time of each attendance upon a safe deposit box. In certain circumstances it might be appropriate to seek a copy of such record, although, since it would probably not be within the power of the respondent, the issue of a subpoena duces tecum or more probably an application for an inspection appointment would be an obvious alternative.]

Share option scheme   B40

Does the Respondent have the actual or potential benefit of any share option scheme [whether arising from his previous or present employment]? If so, please give full particulars, quantifying such benefit so far as possible, with supporting documentary evidence.

[or, for example]

[As to the share of option scheme referred to in paragraph 8 of the Respondent's affidavit:

(a) Please provide a copy thereof together with copies of any correspondence passing between the Respondent and his employers relating thereto or to any other such scheme(s) of which the Respondent has had or may have the benefit.

(b) What are the Respondent's intentions as to the exercise of the option, given that such exercise will be permitted with effect from the 1st June 2001 and the shares in the company now stand at £1.42 a share more than the option price?

(c) Explain the tax treatment of the scheme.]

Tax: liabilities claimed by respondent   B41

The Respondent asserts that he owes the Inland Revenue £_____. Please produce detailed computations supporting these figures prepared and/or authenticated by the Respondent's accountants.

Tax: potential capital gains   B42

What, according to the Respondent's accountants, would be the Capital Gains Tax for which he would become liable in the event of his disposing of:

(a) the parties' holiday home in Cornwall;

(b) his shareholding in the Hitech Company Limited; and

(c) his collection of paintings.

Tax: principal private residence exemption   B43

Please clarify whether the Respondent has elected to treat _____
as his principal private residence. If so, produce a copy of the document(s) by
which such election was made. What, according to his accountants, is the position
as to the availability of the extra-statutory concession D6?

Trust interests   B44

As to the family trust referred to in the Respondent's affidavit, please produce:

(a) a copy of the trust deed and all subsequent deeds;

(b) copies of the trust accounts for the last three available years;

(c) documentary evidence in the form of a schedule prepared or authenticated
     by one of the trustees of all capital advanced to the Respondent from
     either trust since the creation thereof; and

(d) an estimate of the income and, if applicable, further capital advances
     which the Respondent can reasonably expect to receive from the trusts in
     the foreseeable future.

B(b) Specimen directions

Affidavit: [application for] order to file   **B51**

The Respondent do make, file and serve a copy of an affidavit as to _____ within [14 days of the date of the order to be made on this application].

Affidavit: [application] where enforcement proceedings will probably be necessary   **B53**

1. The Respondent do make, file and serve a copy of an affidavit as to _____ within 14 days of the date of the order to be made on this application.

2. In the event of the Respondent failing to do so, he do make, file and serve a copy of such an affidavit within 14 days of the date upon which the order to be made on this application shall be served on him endorsed with the penal notice.

1 Enforcement proceedings cannot be brought in relation to a mandatory order unless personal service has been effected within the time limit for compliance. If the time limit expires, the order can never be enforced. A second leg is therefore necessary to ensure the order cannot go out of date.

Affidavit: narrative   **B53**

The Respondent do [have leave to] file and serve on the Petitioner an affidavit limited to:

> Contributions to the marriage;
> Conduct;
> [*as appropriate*]

The affidavit be filed and a copy served by _____ 20_____ [and, if the Respondent does not intend to file such an affidavit, he do give notice to the Petitioner by _____ 20_____].

1 Such an affidavit will often be required in a case which does not settle at the Financial Dispute Resolution appointment (*W v. W (Ancillary Relief: Practice)* [2000] Fam. Law 473).

Affidavit: leave if so advised   B54

The Respondent do have leave if so advised to file and serve on the Petitioner an affidavit as to _____ within 14 days and, if he does not intend to do so, he do give notice to the Petitioner within 14 days.

Affidavits: simultaneous exchange   B55

The Petitioner and Respondent do each file and serve on the other an affidavit limited to:

[*as appropriate*]

The affidavits must be filed at court and copies simultaneously exchanged by _____ 20 _____.

Questionnaire   B56

The Respondent do by _____ 20_____ reply to [questions numbered _____ contained in] the Petitioner's questionnaire dated _____ 20 _____.

Questionnaire: where not yet served   B57

Upon the Petitioner undertaking through her solicitors by _____ 20 _____ to serve on the Respondent a list of such questions as she wishes to put to him relating to _____, the Respondent do by _____ 20 _____ saving all just exceptions provide the documents and information requested.

1 This formula is rarely appropriate in an application for directions. It is, however, sometimes used by district judges with a view to maintaining the momentum of the litigation. Its effect is that, if the Respondent objects to any particular question on the basis, for example, that it is oppressive or unnecessary, he should state the objection in the answers to the questionnaire; but, subject to such objection, the questionnaire must be answered within the period specified. As to the questions objected to, the onus shifts to the applicant to restore the matter to the district judge for further directions.

Provision of particular documents   B58

The Respondent do by _____ 20 _____ serve on the Petitioner copies of the documents:

requested in the letter(s) dated _____ 20____;
listed in the schedule(s) dated _____ 20 _____;
[*as appropriate*]

Disclosure of documents by list   B59

Each party do by _____ 20_____ make, serve and file a list of the documents which are or have been in his or her possession, custody or power and accounting for the same and do, within 7 days after service of such list, on reasonable notice, produce to the other party or his or her solicitor such of the said documents as by such list shall appear to be in his or her possession, custody or power except such of them as he or she may in the said list object to produce and that the other party or his or her solicitor be at liberty to inspect and peruse the documents so produced and to take copies and abstracts thereof and extracts therefrom at his or her own expense.

Experts' evidence   B60

1. Both the Petitioner and the Respondent do have leave to adduce expert [accountants'] evidence, such evidence to be limited to one witness on behalf of each party [, namely _____ on behalf of the Petitioner and _____ on behalf of the Respondent].

2. The reports of the said [accountants] shall be in writing and shall be disclosed by simultaneous exchange by _____ 20_____.

[3. The amount of the experts' fees recoverable by one party from the other shall not exceed £_____ including VAT and disbursements.]

1 Family Proceedings Rules 1991, r. 2.61C, applying Civil Procedure Rules 1998, Part 35.

Experts' evidence: experts to confer   B61

1. The parties do have leave to instruct _____ expert(s) each for the purpose of reporting as to _____.

2. Reports shall be disclosed by simultaneous exchange by _____ 20_____.

3. Leave is conditional upon the experts confirming in writing to the court within 14 days from this order that they are prepared and able to comply with the directions herein. The court directs that the expert witnesses discuss the areas of dispute revealed by the reports within 21 days of disclosure and where possible agree on any issue. Within 21 days of such discussion, an agreed statement signed

by the experts stating the issues which are agreed and those which are not agreed and the reasons for disagreement shall be simultaneously disclosed to the parties and a copy shall be filed at court by _____ 20_____.

Joint valuation   B62

1. The parties do forthwith consult for the purpose of jointly instructing expert(s) to report on the value of _____.

2. In default of agreement as to who shall be instructed, he be nominated by the [President for the time being of the Royal Institution of Chartered Surveyors].

3. The costs of the joint valuation be in the first instance borne by [the parties in equal shares] [and shall not exceed £_____ including VAT and disbursements].

4. If possible, joint instructions should be agreed and delivered by _____ 20_____. In default of agreement, each party may deliver instructions by _____ 20_____ and copies of any instructions delivered must at the same time be sent to the other party.

5. Copies of the joint instructions and the report shall be filed with the court by _____ 20_____.

1 A joint valuation will not be irrevocably binding on the parties (*Brent v. Brent* (1978) 9 Fam Law 59 and *Daniels v. Walker* (*Practice Note*) [2000] 1 W.L.R. 1382). It follows that either party can seek leave to adduce further expert evidence under Civil Procedure Rules 1998, r. 35.4 (applied by Family Proceedings Rules 1991, r. 2.61C.

Service on third parties   B63

A copy of the Petitioner's application for variation of the A.B. Smith 1964 Marriage Settlement and a copy of her affidavit dated _____ 20_____ be served on the following beneficiaries under the Settlement, namely John Edward Smith and Jane Jennifer Cooper, and that the said John Edward Smith and Jane Jennifer Cooper do have leave to file affidavits in answer or otherwise in response to the said application within 14 days after service.

1 Family Proceedings Rules 1991, r. 2.59.

Intervener   B64

1. _____ be at liberty to intervene in this application.

2. The said intervener do by _____ 20_____ make and file an affidavit and serve a copy of the same on the Petitioner and the Respondent.

3. The Petitioner and the Respondent each do by _____ 20_____ make, file and serve a copy of an affidavit in answer.

Pensions   B65

The Respondent do forthwith request a valuation under Regulation 4 of the Divorce etc. Pensions Regulations 1996 from the trustees or managers of his pension scheme and serve copies on the Petitioner within 7 days of receipt.

1 Family Proceedings Rules 1991, r. 2.61D(2)(f)(iii).

Pensions: where difficulties are expected   B66

The Respondent do request the trustees or managers of any pension scheme under which he has or is likely to have benefits to provide a valuation under Regulation 4 of the Divorce etc. (Pensions) Regulations 1996 and to state in writing what proportion of the estimated cash equivalent or value of the Respondent's rights is in their opinion attributable to any pension or other periodical payment under such scheme(s) to which the Petitioner would or might become entitled in the event of the Respondent's death. In this order:

(a) the expression "pension scheme" includes:

  (i) a retirement annuity contract; or
  (ii) an annuity, or insurance policy, purchased or transferred for the purpose of giving effect to rights under a pension scheme;

(b) in relation to such a contract or annuity, the reference to the trustees or managers shall be read as a reference to the provider of the annuity;

(c) in relation to such a policy, the reference to the trustees or managers shall be read as a reference to the insurer;

(d) in the case of an occupational pension scheme, the expression "valuation" shall mean the information mentioned in Regulation 6(7) of, and paragraphs 8 and 9 of Schedule 2 to, the Occupational Pension Schemes (Disclosure of Information) Regulations 1986;

(e) in the case of a personal pension scheme, the expression "valuation" shall mean the information mentioned in paragraph 2(a) (or, where applicable, paragraph 2(b)) of Schedule 2 to the Personal Pension Schemes (Disclosure of Information) Regulations 1987.

1 See Family Proceedings Rules 1991, r. 2.71, Matrimonial Causes Act 1973, s.25D and the Divorce etc. (Pensions) Regulations 1996, regs 4 and 5. These three statutory authorities are also set out in the specimen letter to the trustees of a pension scheme in precedent B3(k) in the main work.

2 Divorce etc. (Pensions) Regulations 1996, reg. 4(4) imposes an obligation on the trustees to furnish the information and valuation under reg. 4 where the Respondent requests it or where he has been required by the court to request it. The district judge, however, has no specific power to order the Respondent to request a valuation of the spouse's rights under reg. 5. However, it is submitted that, on the authority of *G v. G (Financial Discovery)* [1991] F.C.R. 808 (where it was held that a district judge can order a party to use his best endeavours to obtain information from a third party), the district judge can nonetheless order the Respondent to make a request under reg. 5, although the trustees are not obliged to furnish the information if the Respondent disobeys the order.

Scott Schedule   B67

1. The parties do complete a Scott Schedule, drawn in appropriately numbered columns, stating in relation to each disputed chattel each party's case as to:

(a) The party by whom it was acquired;

(b) The manner of acquisition, for example "purchase" or "inheritance from mother" or as the case may be;

(c) Its present value;

(d) What order the court should be asked to make.

2. Each party shall, when completing the Schedule, prepare and send to the other a paginated bundle containing documents relevant to the questions of acquisition, ownership and value of each chattel and the Schedule shall be cross-referenced to the bundle.

3. The Schedule shall also contain a right-hand column for the use of the court.

4. The Petitioner do by _____ 20____ complete and serve on the Respondent's solicitors the Schedule and her bundle of documents.

5. Within 14 days of service, the Respondent do complete and serve on the Petitioner's solicitors the Schedule and his bundle of documents.

HM Land Registry entries   B68

The Petitioner do by _____ 20____ obtain, file and serve on the Respondent's solicitors up-to-date office copies of the entries on the Register at HM Land Registry relating to _____.

Bankers' books   B69

1. The Petitioner be at liberty to inspect and take copies of books and records of _____ Bank PLC, namely:

(a) the bank statements for the past three years in respect of all the Respondent's accounts;

(b) the payees of the following cheques: _____

2. Such inspection and taking of copies shall be permitted by the _____ Bank PLC not later than 7 days after service of this order upon it.

1 Bankers' Books Evidence Act 1879, s. 7: "On the application of any party to a legal proceeding a court or judge may order that such party be at liberty to inspect and take copies of any entries in a banker's book for any of the purposes of such proceedings. An order under this section may be made either with or without summoning the bank or any other party, and shall be served on the bank three clear days before the same is to be obeyed, unless the court or judge otherwise directs."

2 By s. 9 of the Act the expression "bank" includes a building society, the National Savings Bank and the Post Office. The court may make an order in respect of a bank in Scotland or Northern Ireland (*Kissam v. Link* [1986] 1 Q.B. 574).

3 Cheques and credit slips are not records of the bank subject to inspection under the Act (*Williams v. Williams* [1988] Q.B. 161).

4 An application for an order under the Act is normally, but not necessarily, made on notice to the other party and supported by an affidavit. The bank is not required to be served with the notice of the application.

Inspection appointment   B70

_____ do attend at the _____ County Court at _____ on _____ day the _____ day of _____ 20_____ at o'clock and he do bring with him and produce the documents specified below:

[*as appropriate*]

1 Family Proceedings Rules 1991, r. 2.62(7) to (9).

2 An application is normally made on notice to the other party, but not on notice to the party who is to produce the documents. However, if there is a legitimate anxiety that notice may lead to the destruction of documents, an *ex parte* application may be justified (*B v. B* [1995] 1 F.L.R. 913). An affidavit in support is normally expected.

3 As an alternative to an inspection appointment, a witness summons or subpoena may be applied for. It has been held in the Chancery Division (*Khanna v. Lovell White Durrant (a firm)* [1994] 4 All E.R. 267) that a *subpoena duces tecum* can be served on a non-party requiring his attendance at court on a date before the planned trial date.

4 It is also open to the district judge to order a party to use his best endeavours to obtain specified information from a third party. See *G v. G (Financial Discovery)* [1991] F.C.R. 808.

Financial Dispute Resolution appointment   B71

The application be referred to a Financial Dispute Resolution appointment to take place at _____ on [_____ 20____] [a date to be fixed] [the first open date after _____ 20____].

Financial Dispute Resolution appointment dispensed with   B72

A Financial Dispute Resolution appointment be dispensed with because [the first appointment was treated as such an appointment by consent] [it is inappropriate to this case because _____].

Final hearing   B73

1. The final hearing of the Petitioner's application be listed for hearing by a [District/Circuit/High Court] Judge on _____ at _____ o'clock [or on the first open date after _____ 20____ [suitable to Counsel for both parties]] with a time estimate of _____.

2. Both parties do attend to give oral evidence.

3. Any witness swearing an affidavit do attend the hearing to give oral evidence.

4. The hearing shall not be before District Judge _____.

Bundles   B74

1. The Petitioner do prepare a bundle containing:

   A summary of the history of the case;
   A summary of the issues to be determined;
   A chronology;
   A schedule of the documents included in the bundle;
   The documents, which must include:
      the applications and orders
      Form Es
      other affidavits
      experts' reports
      [as appropriate]

2. The bundle must, if possible, be agreed by both parties.

3. The bundle must be paginated and the documents must be in chronological order within each section.

84

4. The bundle must be filed at court [by _____ 20____] [not later than _____ days before the final hearing].

1 The President's Direction of March 10, 2000 (see A(d)) sets out detailed requirements as to bundles for hearings with a time estimate of half a' day or more. The directions are subject to any specific directions given in a particular case.

Costs estimate   B75

The Petitioner and the Respondent do file and serve on the other costs estimates in Form H not later than [7 days before the final hearing].

Open proposals: no requirement to file   B76

The Petitioner may, if so advised, decline to file and serve an open statement in accordance with rule 2.69E(1). If she shall file and serve such a statement, the Respondent must within 7 days of service file an open statement under rule 2.69E(2).

1 The filing of open proposals under rule 2.69E will be the almost invariable practice. However, there may be cases where it is undesirable. For example, where a Respondent has clearly failed to make proper disclosure or where a substantial difficulty with the evidence cannot be resolved until the hearing, the formulation of open proposals may be an unhelpful or wasteful exercise.

C   Orders

C(a) Specimen clauses for consent orders

Sale of former matrimonial home: agreement   **C2**

Upon the Petitioner and Respondent agreeing and upon their undertaking to the court promptly to take all necessary steps to implement their agreement set out below:

(a) The former matrimonial home _____ shall be sold forthwith and the net proceeds of sale divided [equally between them] [*or* as to _____ % to the Petitioner and _____% to the Respondent].

(b) "Net proceeds of sale" means the gross sale price including any consideration paid for fixtures and fittings less the estate agents' and solicitors' costs and disbursements on sale and the amount necessary to redeem the mortgage to _____ on the basis that the Respondent has made all payments due up to the date of sale.

(c) Messrs _____ or such other agents as may be agreed between the parties or shall in default of agreement be determined by the court shall be instructed in the sale.

(d) The price shall be as agreed between the parties or failing agreement as advised by the agents instructed in the sale [*or* as may be determined by the court].

(e) The _____'s solicitors shall be instructed in the sale [at a fee agreed, subject to unforeseen circumstances, at £_____ plus VAT and disbursements].

1 In appropriate circumstances this may be the subject of a court order, rather than contained in the preamble to a court order. See note to C54.

Sale of matrimonial home: one party to receive a fixed sum from the proceeds of sale   **C3**

Upon the Petitioner and Respondent agreeing and upon their undertaking to the court promptly to take all necessary steps to implement their agreement set out below:

(a) The former matrimonial home _____ shall be sold forthwith and the proceeds of sale divided as to £_____ to the Petitioner and the balance to the Respondent.

(b) The sum of £＿＿ referred to in the immediately preceding paragraph shall be increased by £＿＿ a day for each day by which completion of the sale is delayed after ＿＿＿＿＿＿＿.

(c) Subject to the next following sub-paragraph, the Respondent shall have the conduct of the sale and shall be entitled to decide the price.

(d) This sub-paragraph shall have effect if contracts for the sale shall not have been exchanged by ＿＿＿＿＿＿＿ with completion no later than six weeks thereafter. All matters connected with the sale, including the price, shall be decided by agreement between the parties and, if there shall be any dispute, any such dispute shall be settled by a surveyor agreed between the parties and in default of agreement appointed by the President for the time being of the Royal Institution of Chartered Surveyors; and such surveyor may act in the sale.

(e) The Respondent shall make all payments in respect of the mortgage to ＿＿＿＿＿＿＿ due up to the date of sale [or the Petitioner shall make all payments in respect of the mortgage to ＿＿＿＿＿＿＿ due up to the date of sale and in the event of there being any arrears at the date of sale, such arrears shall be deducted from the sum of £＿＿ hereinbefore referred to].

Sale of matrimonial home: where the sale is to coincide with the petitioner's new purchase   C4

Upon the Petitioner and Respondent agreeing and upon their undertaking to the court promptly to take all necessary steps to implement their agreement set out below:

(a) The former matrimonial home ＿＿＿＿＿＿ shall be sold and the net proceeds of sale divided equally between the parties [or as to ＿＿＿ % to the Petitioner and ＿＿＿% to the Respondent].

(b) "Net proceeds of sale" means the gross proceeds of sale including any consideration paid for fixtures and fittings less the estate agents' and solicitors' costs and disbursements on sale and the amount necessary to redeem the mortgage to ＿＿＿＿＿＿ on the basis that the Respondent has made all payments due up to the date of sale.

(c) Exchange of contracts and completion of the sale shall be arranged so far as is reasonable to coincide with the purchase by the Petitioner of a new property to live in, upon the Petitioner undertaking to the court that she will use all diligence in seeking and buying such new property.

1 Such other terms from the immediately preceding precedents as are appropriate should be added.

Undertaking to guarantee mortgage C5

Upon the Respondent undertaking [if and only if it shall be necessary to enable the Petitioner to obtain borrowing on reasonable terms] to guarantee a mortgage of up to £____ to be taken out by the Petitioner on her proposed purchase of _____, provided that, if she shall default in making any of the payments due under the said mortgage and the Respondent shall be called upon to make any payments under the said guarantee, she shall indemnify him in respect of any liability [and that he shall be entitled to deduct the same from the periodical payments due to the Petitioner under the terms of this order].

And upon the Petitioner undertaking forthwith in the event of her remarriage [or in the event that she shall have cohabited with another man for a continuous period of six months] to take all such steps as shall be necessary to procure the release of the Respondent from all liability under the said guarantee [and upon the Petitioner further undertaking from time to time upon the Respondent reasonably so requesting to use her reasonable endeavours to procure the Respondent's release].

Transfer of matrimonial home: petitioner buying out respondent at an agreed figure C6

Upon the Petitioner and Respondent agreeing as follows:

(a) The Petitioner shall buy and the Respondent shall sell all that the right and interest of the Respondent in the former matrimonial home _____ [and in any management, residents' or other similar company or association].

(b) Completion shall take place on or before _____.

(c) The consideration shall be £____ plus £____ for each day by which completion shall be delayed after _____ save insofar as such delay may be attributable to the Respondent or his advisers.

(d) Time shall be of the essence.

And upon the Petitioner undertaking to the court [from time to time upon the Respondent reasonably so requesting] to use all reasonable endeavours to ensure that the Respondent is released from all liability in respect of the mortgage to

_____ and in the meantime to indemnify him against any liability in respect of the said mortgage.

Outgoings: undertaking by the party not in occupation   C7

Upon the Respondent undertaking to the court for so long as the Petitioner shall be entitled to periodical payments for herself promptly to make all payments due in respect of the mortgage to _____ on the former matrimonial home _____ and promptly to pay the accounts relating to the following outgoings on the said former matrimonial home, namely, general rates, water rates, gas, electricity, telephone, fabric insurance and contents insurance, until such time as the said former matrimonial home shall be sold or further order.

Former matrimonial home: withdrawal of notice of rights of occupation   C8

Upon the Petitioner undertaking to the court to take all steps forthwith to procure the cancellation of the registration of her matrimonial home rights under the Family Law Act 1996 and not to make any application under the Family Law Act 1996 for an order in respect of the said former matrimonial home.

Leasehold property: indemnity by spouse in occupation   C9

Upon the Petitioner undertaking to the court to comply with the terms of the lease of _____ and to indemnify the Respondent in respect of any liability arising in respect of the said lease.

General waiver of claims   C10

Upon the parties agreeing that [subject to implementation of this order] neither has any claim, or shall in respect of or arising out of their marriage or its dissolution or their relationship as spouses or former spouses make any claim in the future, against the other or against the estate of the other, whether in England and Wales or elsewhere.

1 Provided that there is a waiver of property claims (see C13) and a dismissal of claims (see C67 _et seq._), such a clause is seldom necessary except where it may be of evidential use in cases with a foreign element.

Waiver of claim to specified asset   C11

Upon the Respondent acknowledging that he has no beneficial interest in _____.

[or]

Upon the parties agreeing that the _____ is the absolute property of the Petitioner.

Chattels: agreed division of matrimonial home contents   C12

Upon the parties agreeing that the items [set out on the list lodged herewith and marked "A" or set out in the schedule hereto or set out on the list enclosed with the letter from the Petitioner's solicitors to the Respondent's solicitors dated _____ or as the case may be] are the absolute property of the Respondent and the remaining contents of the former matrimonial home are the absolute property of the Petitioner.

And upon both parties acknowledging that, subject to collection by the Respondent of the said items, neither has any claim against the other in respect of property including for the avoidance of doubt but not limited to any claim under section 17 of the Married Women's Property Act 1882 as amended and extended.

MWPA 1882, section 17: waiver of claims   C13

And upon both parties acknowledging that neither has any claim against the other in respect of property including for the avoidance of doubt but not limited to any claim under section 17 of the Married Women's Property Act 1882 as amended and extended.

MWPA 1882, section 17: waiver of claims conditional upon the parties having divided the contents of the former matrimonial home   C14

Upon both parties agreeing and acknowledging that, subject to their agreeing and implementing a division of the contents of the matrimonial home _____, neither has any claim against the other in respect of property including for the avoidance of doubt but not limited to any claim under section 17 of the Married Women's Property Act 1882 as amended and extended [and that, upon agreement or adjudication by the court in respect of the said contents, they will each consent to an order dismissing their respective claims for property adjustment orders, those claims being kept alive solely for the purpose of giving the court jurisdiction to effect a division of the said contents].

1 The distinction between the declaratory jurisdiction under section 17 of the Married Women's Property Act 1882 and the adjustive jurisdiction under section 24 of the Matrimonial Causes Act 1973 must be borne in mind.

2 The final leg of this precedent would be included where the parties' property adjustment claims were being left open for the purpose of determining an issue as to the division of chattels. Otherwise, the party with the greater need for chattels, for example to furnish a home for the children, might be unable to secure a proper division.

Insurance cover: undertaking to take out and maintain a policy   C15

Upon the Respondent undertaking to the court that he will forthwith take out with a reputable United Kingdom insurance company a policy on his life in the sum of £_____ [with/without profits] for [the term of _____ years/the whole of his life] for the benefit of the Petitioner and that until the Petitioner's death or earlier remarriage he will promptly pay all premiums due and will take all steps to ensure that the said policy shall remain in full force, [*in the case, for example, of a policy capable of acquiring a surrender value, add, if appropriate*] the parties having agreed that, if the Petitioner shall remarry or shall predecease the Respondent, the Respondent [*or as the case may be*] shall be entitled to the benefit of the policy.

1 Following decree absolute a party does not have an insurable interest in the life of the other, except, arguably, to the extent necessary to replace maintenance. This precedent envisages the policy being written on trust on the terms set out. The next precedent provides for a simple assignment of the new policy.

2 If the order also provides for dismissal of claims, consideration should be given to providing that the dismissal does not take effect until the policy has been taken out. It would not normally be appropriate for the dismissal to be dependent on compliance with a continuing undertaking to pay premiums.

3 It may be desirable to include an undertaking to authorise the insurance company from time to time to provide information to the Petitioner about the policy. See C17.

Insurance cover: undertaking to take out and assign a policy   C16

Upon the Respondent undertaking to the court that he will forthwith take out with [the _____ Insurance Company Limited [a reputable United Kingdom insurance company] a policy on his life [with/without profits] for [the term of _____ years/the whole of his life] and forthwith assign it absolutely to the Petitioner, she being responsible for the payment of all premiums.

1 See the note to precedent C15.

Insurance cover: undertaking to give authority to insurance company to divulge information $\quad$ C17

Upon the Respondent undertaking to the court forthwith [upon taking out of the policy referred to in the immediately preceding paragraph] irrevocably to author-ise the _____ Insurance Company Limited [or the company with whom the said policy shall have been taken out] to disclose to the Petitioner such information as she may from time to time request relating to policy number _____ [or such policy].

Covenant to leave by will $\quad$ C18

Upon the Respondent undertaking and, in consideration of the arrangements contained in this order, agreeing, such agreement to be binding on his estate, that he will leave by will to the Petitioner in the event that she shall survive him not having remarried and not having had her claim for periodical payments dismissed by the court, the sum of £____ [increased in proportion with the rise in the Retail Prices Index between _____ 20____ and the month of the Respon-dent's death] [less any monies paid to her under the Respondent's pension scheme on his death or under any life policy or other such arrangement effected by the Respondent].

1 If time permits, it would be preferable to draft a deed of covenant. See C19.

Undertaking to execute deed $\quad$ C19

Upon the Respondent undertaking [within _____ days of decree absolute] to execute and deliver to the Petitioner a deed in the form of the draft attached marked "A".

Medical insurance $\quad$ C20

Upon the Respondent undertaking to the court to pay for medical insurance with _____ for the Petitioner until she shall remarry and for the children of the family _____ until [they shall respectively cease their secondary education] at [specify scale of cover, e.g. no lower level (of cover, not of cost) than now].

100

Medical insurance: employer's scheme   C21

Upon the Respondent undertaking to the court to ensure that [the Petitioner until she shall remarry and] the children of the family _____ are covered by such medical insurance scheme as his employers shall from time to time arrange [provided that such covering shall be at no cost to the Respondent save any additional charge to income tax].

Pension scheme: nomination to receive death in service benefit   C22

Upon the Respondent undertaking to the court forthwith to nominate the Petitioner and, for so long as she shall not have remarried and provided she shall be living at his death, to keep her nominated to receive [not less than _____ % of] the death in service benefit payable under such pension scheme or schemes as he shall from time to time be a member of, [subject to a maximum of _____ times the annual amount of the periodical payments due to her for herself immediately before his death,] [provided that in the event of his remarrying such nomination shall be as to not less than _____% of the said benefit, [subject to a maximum of _____ times the said annual amount,]] and forthwith to provide written evidence of the receipt by the trustees or managers of such scheme or schemes of such nomination.

1 Although the court has the power in most cases to make an order under Matrimonial Causes Act 1973, s. 25C for the payment of the death in service benefit to the other party, such an order will not cover a new pension scheme except to the extent to which transfer credits are derived from the first scheme (see Matrimonial Causes Act 1973, s. 25D(1)). In appropriate cases such an order (see precedent C57) might also be sought as a belt and braces measure. The advantage of an order is that, where a nomination is not binding on the pension fund trustees (as is normally the case), the order will bind the trustees. This effectively prevents the nomination being secretly altered.

2 It will seldom be practicable for there to be an undertaking to submit to a further court order under the Matrimonial Causes Act 1973, s. 25C in respect of a later scheme, for most negotiated settlements will provide for a dismissal of further lump sum claims.

School fees: undertaking   C23

Upon the Respondent undertaking to the court promptly to pay the school fees [and any extras on the bill *or* such extras as shall have been agreed in advance between the parties] for the children of the family _____ [at such schools as the said children shall by agreement between the Petitioner and the Respondent or by order of the court attend] [insofar as the said school fees [and extras] exceed [£_____ a term/the amount received under policy number _____ with _____]].

1 Although commonly covered by an undertaking, there is no reason why educational expenses should not be payable under a court order. See C36 and C37.

Company: resignation and transfer of shares C24

Upon the Petitioner undertaking:

(a) Forthwith to resign as Director/Company Secretary of _____ Limited.

(b) Forthwith to transfer to the Respondent all her shares in the said company [*or* all that her title to and interest in any shares in the said company].

AND upon the Petitioner acknowledging that she has no claim against the said company.

AND upon the Respondent undertaking to indemnify the Petitioner and her estate in respect of any losses, claims, demands or other liabilities arising from her involvement with the said company including but without prejudice to the generality of the foregoing any Capital Gains Tax arising on the transfer by the Petitioner of her shareholding in the said company to the Respondent in accordance with her undertaking given above, any other tax liability that may be incurred by the Petitioner as a result of her involvement in the said company whether in respect of fees, dividends or otherwise and any professional fees incurred by the Petitioner in respect thereof.

1 Depending on the company and the Petitioner's involvement in it, it may be appropriate for there to be an exchange of letters between the company and the Petitioner confirming that neither has any claim against the other.

2 Alternatively, a transfer of property order could provide for the transfer of shares.

Record of intention where continuing provision (e.g. payment of endowment policy premiums) is intended to be part of the capital provision for the recipient. C25

Upon the parties recording that the undertaking by the Respondent to _____ is part of the capital provision agreed to be made for the Petitioner and is therefore intended to be irrevocable during the joint lives of the parties irrespective of any change in circumstances including the Petitioner's remarriage.

1 See notes to precedent C26.

Record of intention not to seek variation C26

Upon the Petitioner recording that it is not her intention to seek a variation of the periodical payments hereinafter ordered [except if she shall have to cease employment because of ill-health *or* for the period of _____ years from the date of this order *or as the case may be*].

1 Matrimonial Causes Act 1973, s. 34(1)(a) provides that an agreement purporting to restrict a right to apply to the court for an order containing financial arrangements shall be void. Neither can the parties attempt by agreement to fetter the discretion of the court (*Jessel v. Jessel* [1979] 3 All E.R. 645). Such an agreement, however, may well have evidential value.

2 The court will not accept an undertaking and usually the best that can be done is to record the parties' intentions.

Inheritance Etc. Act 1975: record of intention to limit claims C27

Upon the Petitioner acknowledging that in the event of the Respondent pre-deceasing her any claim that she may make against his estate under the Inheritance (Provision for Family and Dependants) Act 1975 shall be limited to seeking a sum or sums in compensation for the loss to her of the income provision hereinafter ordered.

1 See note to precedent C26.

Costs: undertaking not to enforce C28

Upon the Petitioner undertaking to the Court not to seek to enforce the order for costs herein made on _____ 20____.

Get: agreement to obtain C29

Upon both parties undertaking to the Court to take all steps necessary to obtain a Get as soon as practicable, all expenses in connection therewith to be paid by the _____.

Maintenance pending suit: order C30

The Respondent do pay or cause to be paid to the Petitioner with effect from _____ until further order maintenance pending suit at the rate of £____ a year payable monthly [in advance].

1 Matrimonial Causes Act 1973, s. 22.

2 The payments may not start earlier than the date of the presentation of the petition nor continue after the determination of the suit, *i.e.* decree absolute. If the payments are backdated, the order, or the preamble to the order, should stipulate when the arrears are to be paid.

3 There is no jurisdiction to make a maintenance pending suit order after decree absolute (*M v. M* [1928] P. 123). If the order is being made after decree absolute the payments may start earlier than decree absolute (subject to the restriction imposed by Matrimonial Causes Act 1973, s. 28(1) (see note 2 to C32), but will be described as periodical payments rather than maintenance pending suit.

4 Payments are to be made in arrears unless the order specifies that they are to be made in advance.

Maintenance pending suit followed by interim periodical payments   C31

The Respondent do pay or cause to be paid to the Petitioner [interim] maintenance pending suit with effect from _____ until decree absolute and thereafter interim periodical payments during joint lives until she shall remarry or further order at the rate of £____ a year payable monthly [in advance].

1 Family Proceedings Rules 1991, r. 2.64(2).

2 An order in this form can only be made between decree nisi and decree absolute, for maintenance pending suit cannot be made after decree absolute and an order for periodical payments cannot be made until decree nisi (see notes to precedent C30).

Periodical payments: order (or interim order) to spouse   C32

The Respondent do make or cause to be made to the Petitioner with effect from _____ during joint lives until she shall remarry or further order [interim] periodical payments at the rate of £____ a year payable monthly [in advance].

1 Matrimonial Causes Act 1973, s. 23(1)(a).

2 The order may not start earlier than the date of the making of the application (which may be an appropriate prayer in a petition or answer) and shall not extend beyond the death of either party or the remarriage of the payee (Matrimonial Causes Act 1973, s. 28(1)(a)). If the payments are backdated, the order, or the preamble to the order, should stipulate when the arrears are to be paid.

3 Payments are to be made in arrears unless the order specifies that they are to be made in advance.

Periodical payments: order to or for child   C33

The Respondent do make or cause to be made to [the Petitioner for the benefit of] [each of] the child[ren] of the family _____ with effect from _____ until [he/she/they] shall [respectively] attain the age of 17 years or shall cease [secondary education *or* to receive full–time education or to undergo training for a trade, profession or vocation] whichever shall be the later or further order [interim] periodical payments at the rate of £____ a year payable monthly [in advance].

1 Matrimonial Causes Act 1973, s. 23(1)(d).

2 Child Support Act 1991, s. 8(5) provides: "The Lord Chancellor ... may by order provide that, in such circumstances as may be specified by the order, this section shall not prevent a court from exercising any power which it has to make a maintenance order in relation to a child if—

   (a) a written agreement (whether or not enforceable) provides for the making, or securing, by an absent parent of the child of periodical payments to or for the benefit of the child; and
   (b) the maintenance order which the court makes is, in all material respects, in the same terms as that agreement."

3 The Child Maintenance (Written Agreements) Order 1993, art. 2 provides: "Section 8 shall not prevent a court from exercising any power which it has to make a maintenance order in relation to a child in any circumstances in which paragraphs (a) and (b) of section 8(5) apply." For most courts, the consent notice of application will be sufficient evidence of the written agreement (see [1995] Fam. Law 460). Other courts may require the parties personally to sign the consent application and/or to include a recital in the consent application along the lines of: "Upon the parties having reached a written agreement within the terms of section 8(5) of the Child Support Act 1991 for periodical payments as hereafter set out."

4 Payments are to be made in arrears unless the order specifies that they are to be made in advance.

5 For tax purposes, except in the very limited circumstances referred to in note 1 to C5-021 in the main work, it now makes no difference whether the payments are to or for a child.

Periodical payments: order to child where special circumstances   C34

The Respondent do make or cause to be made to the child of the family _____ with effect from _____ until further order periodical payments at the rate of £____ a year payable monthly [in advance] it appearing to the court that there are special circumstances which justify the making of an order without complying with the provisions of paragraph (b) of subsection (2) of section 29 of the Matrimonial Causes Act 1973 [*or, if the child has already attained 18* it appearing to the court that there are special circumstances which justify the making of an order without complying with the provisions of subsection (1) and paragraph (b) of subsection (2) of section 29 of the Matrimonial Causes Act 1973].

1 See the notes to precedent C33 and see Matrimonial Causes Act 1973, s. 29(3).

2 An order can also be made in circumstances where the Child Support Agency fixes the child's general maintenance, but it must be limited to what is necessary to cover the child's disability. Child Support Act 1991, s. 8 provides:

"(8) This section shall not prevent a court from exercising any power which it has to make a maintenance order in relation to a child if—

(a) a disability living allowance is paid to or in respect of him; or
(b) no such allowance is paid but he is disabled,

and the order is made solely for the purpose of requiring the person making or securing the making of periodical payments fixed by the order to meet some or all of any expenses attributable to the child's disability.

(9) For the purposes of subsection (8), a child is disabled if he is blind, deaf or dumb or is substantially and permanently handicapped by illness, injury, mental disorder or congenital deformity or such other disability as may be prescribed."

For the avoidance of doubt an order for maintenance where there is already a Child Support Agency assessment should state that the payments are in addition to such payments as may be payable under any assessment.

Periodical payments: order for child (a top up of Child Support Agency assessment) C35

(a) [an] assessment[s] determined by reference to the alternative formula mentioned in paragraph 4(3) of Schedule 1 to the Child Support Act 1991 has [have] been made in respect of the child[ren] _____; and

(b) the court is satisfied that the circumstances of the case make it appropriate for the Respondent to make periodical payments as hereinafter ordered in addition to the child support maintenance payable in accordance with the said assessment.

By consent it is ordered that the Respondent do make or cause to be made to [the Petitioner for the benefit of] [each of] the child[ren] of the family _____ with effect from _____ until [he/she/they] shall [respectively] attain the age of 17 years or shall cease [secondary education *or* to receive full-time education or to undergo training for a trade, profession or vocation], whichever shall be the later, or until further order periodical payments in addition to such payments as shall be due under any assessment made under the Child Support Act 1991 at the rate of £____ a year payable monthly [in advance].

1 This precedent is for use where an assessment has already been made by the Child Support Agency, determined by reference to the alternative formula mentioned in paragraph 4(3) of Schedule 1 to the Act, *i.e.* a high-income case.

Periodical payments: school fees C36

The Respondent do make or cause to be made to the child of the family
_____ with effect from _____ until [he/she] shall attain the
age of 17 years or until [he/she] shall cease to receive full-time education
(whichever is the [later/earlier]) or further order periodical payments for
[himself/herself]:

(a) Of an amount equivalent to the school fees [but not the extras in the school
bill *or* including [such] extras [as have been agreed in advance by the
parties]] at such school as the said child shall by agreement or order of the
court attend for each financial year [by way of three payments on
_____, _____ and _____]; together with

(b) The sum of £____ a year payable monthly in respect of general maintenance of the said child.

[*Add, where desired, for example because it is feared that the other spouse may
dissipate the fees*] And it is further ordered that that part of the order which
reflects the school fees [and said extras] shall be paid to the [Headmaster/Bursar/
School Secretary] as agent for the said child and the receipt of that payee shall be
sufficient discharge.

1 A school fees order can be made not only by consent, but also in contested proceedings.
Child Support Act 1991, s. 8(7) provides: "This section shall not prevent a court from
exercising any power which it has to make a maintenance order in relation to a child if—

(a) the child is, will be or (if the order were to be made) would be receiving instruction
at an educational establishment or undergoing training for a trade, profession or
vocation (whether or not while in gainful employment); and

(b) the order is made solely for the purposes of requiring the person making or securing
the making of periodical payments fixed by the order to meet some or all of the
expenses incurred in connection with the provision of the instruction or training."

However, only leg (a) can be ordered in contested proceedings; general maintenance
would be dealt with by the Child Support Agency. See precedent C37.

Periodical payments: school fees (where Child Support Agency assessment made) C37

The Respondent do make or cause to be made to [the Petitioner for the benefit of]
[each of] the child[ren] of the family _____ with effect from
_____ until such time as [he/she/they] shall respectively cease [second-
ary] education [at _____ School] or until further order periodical
payments in addition to such payments as shall be payable under any assessment
made under the Child Support Act 1991 at the rate of £____ a year payable

monthly [in advance] [*or* of an amount equivalent to [____% of] the school fees [but not the extras on the school bill *or* including reasonable extras] at the school[s] the said child[ren] attend[s] for each financial year by way of three payments on _____, _____, and _____.

[*Add, where desired, for example because it is feared that the other spouse may dissipate the fees*] And it is further ordered that that part of the order which reflects the school fees [and said extras] shall be paid to the [Headmaster/Bursar/School Secretary] as agent for the said child and the receipt of that payee shall be sufficient discharge.

1 See the note to precedent C36.

Periodical payments: global maintenance for wife and child   C38

The Respondent do make or cause to be made to the Petitioner with effect from _____ during joint lives until she shall remarry or further order [interim] periodical payments at the rate of £____ a year payable monthly [in advance] less such sums as may from time to time be payable under any Child Support Agency assessment in respect of the children of the family _____.

1 On a contested basis such an order will only be made if there is a substantial degree of spousal maintenance (*Dorney-Kingdom v. Dorney-Kingdom* [2000] Fam. Law 678).

Periodical payments: wife's order to abate if Child Support Agency assessment made   C39

Whereas the parties have agreed that the provision made hereafter fulfils the Respondent's responsibilities to the child[ren] of the family _____ and it is recorded that the Petitioner does not intend to apply for the revocation of the order for periodical payments for the said child[ren] hereinafter made.

By consent it is ordered that the Respondent do make or cause to be made to the Petitioner with effect from _____ periodical payments payable monthly [in advance] as follows:

(a) for herself during joint lives until she shall remarry or further order at the yearly rate of £____ less the amount by which the amount [*or* the aggregate of the amounts] paid by the Respondent under any assessment[s] made under the Child Support Act 1991 in respect of the said child[ren] _____ shall exceed the periodical payments hereinafter ordered for the benefit of [the said child *or* such children as the assessments shall relate to]; and

(b) for the benefit of [each of] the said child[ren] _____ until [he/she/they] shall [respectively] attain the age of 17 years or shall cease [secondary education *or* to receive full time education or to undergo training for a trade, profession or vocation] whichever shall be the later, or until further order at the yearly rate of £____.

1 As to commencement etc. see C32.

2 Chid Support Act 1991, s. 8(3) provides that where the Child Support Agency has jurisdiction, no court can make, vary or revive a maintenance order in relation to the child and s. 8(4) expressly states that subsection (3) does not prevent a court from revoking a maintenance order.

Periodical payments: order for child where the Child Support Act 1991 applies, for the purpose of giving the court jurisdiction   C40

Upon the parties having agreed:

(a) that the order hereinafter made is for the purpose only of giving the court jurisdiction to make an order for periodical payments for the benefit of the child[ren] of the family _____ as part of an order for ancillary relief to be made on the Petitioner's application dated _____; and

(b) that in the event of the court not making an order on the said application on or before _____, neither party shall oppose an application by the other for the revocation of the order hereinafter made.

By consent it is ordered that the Respondent do make or cause to be made to [the Petitioner for the benefit of] [each of] the child[ren] of the family _____ with effect from _____ until [he/she/they] shall [respectively] attain the age of 17 years or shall cease [secondary education *or* to receive full time education or to undergo training for a trade, profession or vocation], whichever shall be the later, or until further order [interim] periodical payments at the rate of [5p/£____] a year [payable monthly] [in advance].

Periodical payments: index-linking   C41

The periodical payments ordered in paragraph[s] ____ shall, in the event that there shall be any increase in the Retail Prices Index over the 12-month period ending with [*select month, say, three months before the date on which the first payment at the new rate shall be payable*] _____ in any year from and including 20____, be increased by the percentage of such increase with effect from _____ in each such year [*or if the 12-month period ends in the calendar year before the date of the increase* in the year following each such year].

Periodical payments: nominal order   C42

The Respondent do make or cause to be made to the Petitioner during joint lives until she shall remarry or further order periodical payments at the rate of 5p a year.

Periodical payments: fixed term   C43

The Respondent do make or cause to be made to the Petitioner with effect from _____ during joint lives until _____ 20_____ or until her earlier remarriage or further order periodical payments at the rate of £____ a year payable monthly [in advance] and on the expiry of the term specified above the Petitioner's claim[s] for periodical payments [and secured periodical payments] do stand dismissed and it is directed (a) that the Petitioner shall not be entitled to make any further application in relation to the marriage for an order under section 23(1)(a) [or (b)] of the Matrimonial Causes Act 1973 and (b) pursuant to section 28(1A) of that Act that the Petitioner shall not be entitled to apply under section 31 of that Act for an extension of the term specified above.

1 As to commencement and duration see C32.

2 There must be some doubt as to the jurisdictional basis of a dismissal of a periodical payments claim when there has been an order in existence and of a direction under s. 25A(3) in these circumstances (see *Jones v. Jones* (2000) *The Times*, April 11). They have been included out of an abundance of caution. Orders are frequently made in terms similar to these.

Periodical payments: extendable term   C44

The Respondent do make or cause to be made to the Petitioner with effect from _____ during joint lives until _____ 20_____ or until her earlier marriage or further order periodical payments at the rate of £____ a year payable monthly [in advance] and for the avoidance of doubt it is recorded that the Petitioner shall be entitled to apply under section 31 of the Matrimonial Causes Act 1973 for an extension of the term specified above.

1 As to commencement and duration see C32.

2 Although the absence of a bar on extensions under Matrimonial Causes Act 1973, s. 28(1A) is enough to keep alive the court's powers to extend under section 31, it is prudent to make the position clear on the face of the order.

Standing order   C45

The payments required to be made by the Respondent under paragraph _____
shall be made by standing order into the Petitioner's account numbered
_____ with _____ PLC (branch sort code _____)
or such other account as she may from time to time elect.

1 Maintenance Enforcement Act 1991, s. 1 provides that the court may, of its own motion
or on an application made by an interested party, require the payer under a maintenance
order made at a time when the payer was ordinarily resident in England and Wales to
pay by standing order or "by any other method which requires the debtor to give his
authority for payments of a specific amount to be made from an account of his to an
account of the creditor's on specific dates during the period for which the authority is in
force and without the need for further authority from the debtor".

2 Section 1(6) of the Act enables the court to order the payer to open an account. The
court does not have the power, however, to compel a bank to open the account or to
compel the payer to fund it.

Magistrates' court order: order terminating   C46

Pursuant to section 28(1) of the Domestic Proceedings and Magistrates' Courts
Act 1978, the Order of the _____ Magistrates' Court dated
_____ for periodical payments to the _____ do cease to have
effect on _____.

1 Domestic Proceedings and Magistrates' Court Act 1978, s. 28(1) provides: "Where after
the making by a magistrates' court of an order under this Part of this Act proceedings
between, and relating to the marriage of, the parties to the proceedings in which that
order was made have been commenced in the High Court or a county court then, except
in the case of an order for the payment of a lump sum, the court in which the proceedings
or any application made therein are or is pending may, if it thinks fit, direct that the order
made by a magistrates' court shall cease to have effect on such date as may be specified
in the direction."

2 The above provision applies only to orders under Part I of the Act, *i.e.* matrimonial
proceedings in magistrates' courts.

Secured periodical payments: order for spouse   C47

The Respondent do secure to the Petitioner for her life with effect from
_____ until she shall remarry or further order the annual sum of £_____
upon _____ [*or* security to be agreed or referred to the District Judge
in default of agreement] and in default of agreement as to the form of deed, it be
referred to one of the conveyancing counsel of the court to settle the same.

1 As to commencement etc., see the notes to precedent C32.

2 The term of a secured periodical payment order may extend beyond the death of the payer: see Matrimonial Causes Act 1973, s. 28(1)(b).

Charge [or lump sum] to secure repayment of sums paid under Child Support Act 1991 or Social Security Administration Act 1992 C48

The property known as _____ do stand charged in favour of the Respondent as to [or The Petitioner do pay or cause to be paid to the Respondent a lump sum of] an amount equal to the total of all sums hereafter paid by the Respondent:

    (a) under any assessment under the Child Support Act 1991 in respect of the child[ren] _____ [insofar as such sums exceed the monthly equivalent of £____ [(increased with effect from [6th April] in each year starting in 20____ in accordance with any increase in the Retail Prices Index over the preceding 12 months)] [for each child]]; and

    (b) under sections 106 to 108 of the Social Security Administration Act 1992

[together with interest thereon at the rate of ____% [or the rate from time to time in force for judgment debts in the High Court] from [the 6th April next following the date upon which each such sum shall have been paid],] the Respondent's charge not to be enforced until [or the said lump sum to be payable on] the earliest of:

    (a) the death of the Petitioner

    (b) the remarriage of the Petitioner

    (c) the date on which the youngest child to do so shall cease secondary education

    (d) an order of the court

    (e) the sale of the said property

[provided that the amount as to which the said property shall stand charged shall not exceed [for example one half of the gross proceeds of sale of the said property, or, if it shall not have been sold, one half of the gross value, any dispute as to such value to be settled by a surveyor agreed between the parties and in default of agreement appointed by the President for the time being of the Royal Institution of Chartered Surveyors]].

Lump sum order   C49

The Respondent do forthwith [or forthwith upon decree absolute or on _____ [or forthwith on decree absolute if later]] pay to the Petitioner a lump sum of £_____ [, the parties having agreed that time is of the essence and the Respondent acknowledging that it is not his intention to apply to the court for an extension of the time for payment].

1 Matrimonial Causes Act 1973, s. 23(1)(c).

2 A lump sum cannot be payable earlier than decree absolute (Matrimonial Causes Act 1973, s. 23(5).

3 The concluding words of this precedent are an attempt to prevent the Respondent applying to the court to extend the time for payment (see *Masefield v. Alexander* [1995] 1 F.L.R. 100).

4 Where the order is being made in the High Court or is for £5,000 or more in a county court, statutory interest is payable by virtue of the County Court (Interest on Judgment Debts) Order 1991. It is not necessary to provide in the order for interest. Where the order is for less than £5,000 in a county court, see precedent C53.

Lump sum order: secured C50

The Respondent do pay to the Petitioner a lump sum of £_____.01, payable by instalments as follows:

(a) £_____ payable on _____ [or upon decree absolute if later].

(b) 1p payable a day thereafter.

And the said instalments totalling £_____.01 be secured on _____ and, in default of agreement as to the form of instrument or instruments, the matter be referred to one of the conveyancing counsel of the Court for him to settle the same [and it is directed that the decree nisi be not made absolute until the necessary instrument or instruments have been executed].

1 A lump sum can only be secured if it is payable by instalments: Matrimonial Causes Act 1973, s. 23(3)(c).

2 Conveyancing counsel of the court: Matrimonial Causes Act 1973, s. 30.

Lump sum order: instalments with interest under Matrimonial Causes Act 1973, section 23(6) C51

The Respondent do pay to the Petitioner a lump sum of £_____ payable as follows:

(a) £_____ forthwith upon decree absolute.

(b) _____ further instalments of £_____ each payable on _____ and _____.

and that the said further instalments of £_____ do each carry interest at the rate of _____% [or the rate from time to time in force for judgment debts] from [date no *earlier than the date of the order*] _____ until the dates on which the said instalments are respectively due for payment.

1 This precedent is only for use where a lump sum is to be paid by instalments and interest is to be payable for the period *before* the payments are due. See Matrimonial Causes Act 1973, s. 23(6) (inserted by Administration of Justice Act 1982, s. 16).

2 It should be noted that the court has jurisdiction to extend the time for payment of a lump sum and it may be prudent to recite that time is of the essence. See precedent C49.

Lump sum order: "interest" on lump sum of £5,000 or more where it is desired to avoid the restrictions imposed by the County Court (Interest on Judgment Debts) Order 1991, article 4   C52

The Respondent to pay to the Petitioner the following lump sums:

(a) £_____ payable [forthwith upon decree absolute *or* on _____ or forthwith upon decree absolute if later]

(b) In the event that the Respondent shall fail to pay all or any part of the foregoing lump sum by the due date, an amount or amounts equal to [15p] a year for each £1 or part of £1 of any unpaid part calculated and payable on a daily basis from the due date to the date of actual payment less any interest paid by the Respondent under the County Court (Interest on Judgment Debts) Order 1991

the parties having agreed that time is of the essence and the Respondent acknowledging that it is not his intention to apply to the court for an extension of the time for payment.

1 Interest is payable on county court judgments of £5,000 or more. The County Court (Interest on Judgment Debts) Order 1991, art. 4(1) provides: "Where a judgment creditor takes proceedings in a county court to enforce payment under a relevant judgment, the judgment debt shall cease to carry interest thereafter, except where those proceedings fail to produce any payment from the debtor in which case interest shall accrue as if those proceedings had never been taken." This would appear to enable an ingenious judgment debtor to delay payment until the judgment creditor starts enforcement proceedings and then to make a token payment, thereby stopping interest running.

2 A less convoluted alternative is suggested in precedent C53 for lump sums of less than £5,000.

3 As to the concluding words of this precedent, see note 3 to C49.

4 Income tax is payable on interest received. It is debatable whether the "interest" received by the creditor under this order would avoid the charge to income tax.

5 An order in this form may result in the loss of entitlement to statutory interest, for art. 2(2) of the Order provides: "In the case of a judgment or order for the payment of a

judgment debt, other than costs, the amount of which has to be determined at a later date, the judgment debt shall carry interest from that later date."

Lump sum order: "interest" on lump sum of under £5,000   C53

The Respondent do [forthwith upon decree absolute *or* on _____ or forthwith upon decree absolute if later] pay a lump sum calculated as follows:

(a) £____; and

(b) £____ for each day by which payment of the lump sum shall be delayed after _____

the parties having agreed that time is of the essence and the Respondent acknowledging that it is not his intention to apply to the court for an extension of the time for payment.

1 This precedent is for use where there is a payment of less than £5,000 in a county court, such payments not carrying interest statutorily.

Sale of former matrimonial home: order   C54

The former matrimonial home _____ shall be sold forthwith and the net proceeds of sale divided as to ____% to the Petitioner and ____% to the Respondent and it is directed that:

(a) "Net proceeds of sale" means the gross sale price including any consideration paid for fixtures and fittings less the estate agents' and solicitors' costs and disbursements on sale and the amount necessary to redeem the mortgage to _____ on the basis that the Respondent has made all payments due up to the date of sale.

(b) Messrs _____ or such other agents as may be agreed between the parties or shall in default of agreement be determined by the court shall be instructed in the sale.

(c) The price shall be as agreed between the parties and failing agreement as advised by the agents instructed in the sale or as may be determined by the court.

(d) The Petitioner's solicitors shall be instructed in the sale [at a fee agreed, subject to unforeseen circumstances, at £____ plus VAT and disbursements].

1 Orders in this form are frequently made, but the jurisdictional basis is not clear. The statutory code relating to orders for the sale of property is contained in the Matrimonial

Causes Act 1973, s. 24A, which provides for an order to be made on or after the making of an order for secured periodical payments, lump sum or property adjustment. In the absence of such an order, it is arguable that the matter should be dealt with by a recital in the preamble to the court order (see C2).

Pension: periodical payments C55

[Upon the Respondent undertaking to take all steps necessary to take from the [pension policy] referred to in paragraph _____ hereafter sufficient benefits to meet the provision ordered by that paragraph.]

It is ordered that the trustees [or managers] of [the _____ pension scheme or pension policies numbered _____ with _____] do make to the Petitioner with effect [from the date upon which the Respondent shall retire or] from _____ [if later] during the joint lives of the Petitioner and Respondent until she shall remarry or until further order periodical payments [at the rate of £_____ a month or of an amount equal to [one–third] of the Respondent's [net of tax] pension (or, if the Respondent shall have commuted any benefits under the [scheme or policies], the [net of tax] pension he would have received had he not so commuted) from time to time] payable [monthly [in advance] or on the dates on which the Respondent's pension is payable].

1 Matrimonial Causes Act 1973, s. 26B(4).

2 The court has no power to determine when a Respondent should elect to take his retirement or his retirement benefits, or to prevent his commuting. The court can, however, order him to commute: see precedent C56.

Pension: lump sum from commutation C56

[Upon the parties recording that the Respondent's undertaking next referred to is part of the capital provision agreed to be paid to the Petitioner and is therefore intended to be irrevocable during the joint lives of the parties irrespective of any change in circumstances including the Petitioner's remarriage.]

[And upon the Respondent undertaking that he will [not earlier than _____ and not later than _____] [retire and] exercise his right to commute in order to take sufficient benefits to meet the provision ordered by paragraph _____ hereunder.]

[Subject to the Petitioner not having died] [or remarried] The Respondent do [on retirement or on _____] exercise his right to commute [such of] his benefits under [the _____ pension scheme or pension policies numbered _____ with _____] [as will produce [the sum of £_____ or one-third of the lump sum which would be produced if he were to make the maximum permissible commutation]] and the [trustees or manager] of the said [scheme *or* policies] do forthwith pay the said [sum of £_____ *or* one-third] to the Petitioner.

1 Matrimonial Causes Act 1973, s. 25B(4) and (7).

2 Although the court has power to order the Respondent to commute the whole or part of his benefits, Singer J. considered in *T v. T (Financial Relief: Pensions)* [1998] 1 F.L.R. 1072 at 1088 that the court did not have the power to direct *when* he should do so. If the court can be persuaded to fix a date for commutation on a consent application, then all well and good, but it would be prudent in any event to include an undertaking in the preamble to the court order.

3 The court is given the power by Matrimonial Causes Act 1973, s. 31(2)(dd) to vary a pension lump sum order. However, by virtue of section 31(2B), the power disappears on the death of *either* of the parties to the marriage. The words in square brackets at the beginning of the third paragraph should be included if (as will normally be the case) it is not intended that a lump sum should be paid to the estate of a deceased spouse.

Pension: death benefits C57

The trustees of the _____ pension scheme do pay to the Petitioner [50 per cent of] the lump sum payable in respect of the death of the Respondent [provided she shall not have died or remarried before his death].

[or]

The Respondent do nominate the Petitioner and until further order [or until her death or remarriage] do keep her nominated to receive [50 per cent of] the lump sum payable under the _____ pension scheme in respect of his death.

1 Matrimonial Causes Act 1973, s. 25C(1) and (2).

2 The form of the order will depend on whether the trustees (as for tax reasons is normally the case) or the employee has the power to determine who shall receive the lump sum payable in respect of the employee's death.

3 As to the words in square brackets, see note 3 to C56.

Transfer of property: order with dismissal of capital claims C58

The Respondent do forthwith upon decree absolute [*or if decree absolute already made* on or before _____] transfer or cause to be transferred to the Petitioner all that his right and interest in the property known as _____ _____ [subject to the mortgage to _____] [and in any management, residents' or other similar company or association]; and upon such transfer all the Petitioner's claims for secured periodical payments, lump sum or sums and further or other property adjustment orders do stand dismissed and it is directed that she shall not be entitled to make any further application in relation to the marriage for an order under section 23(1)(b) of the Matrimonial Causes Act 1973.

Mesher order   C59

The property known as _____ shall be held by the Petitioner and the Respondent on trust for sale with power to postpone the sale and, pending sale, the Petitioner may occupy the said property to the exclusion of the Respondent during her life until the [youngest of the] child[ren] of the family [to do so] shall have completed full-time secondary education [*or as the case may be*] [and thereafter for so long as the parties shall agree until the court shall otherwise order, the parties having liberty to apply for this purpose] and upon sale to hold the net proceeds upon trust for the Petitioner and Respondent in equal shares [*or as the case may be*].

1 *Mesher v. Mesher and Hall* [1980] 1 All E.R. 126.

2 The court cannot extend the term unless it is clear on the face of the order that this is envisaged. See *Omielan v. Omielan* [1996] 2 F.L.R. 306.

3 Provision should be made as to who will be responsible for the payments on any mortgage and collateral policies, outgoings and repairs and as to all other matters which might be in dispute during the term. Provision may also be made for the term to end upon the remarriage or cohabitation of the petitioner.

4 The parties should also consider what should happen to any endowment policy assigned collaterally with a mortgage. See precedent C61.

Martin order   C60

The property known as _____ be held by the Petitioner and the Respondent upon trust for sale for themselves as beneficial tenants in common in equal shares [*or as the case may be*], such sale to be postponed until the death or remarriage of the Petitioner or until her earlier agreement to the sale of the said property or further order.

1 *Martin v. Martin* [1978] Fam. 12.

2 See the notes to precedent C59.

Collateral life policy: provision relating to proceeds if maturity takes place before sale of property   C61

AND it is further ordered that, if the endowment policy numbered _____ with _____ shall have matured and the proceeds or part thereof paid to the mortgagees of the said property, then the parties' shares of the net proceeds of sale hereinbefore referred to shall be adjusted so that an amount equal to the amount so paid shall be deducted from the said net proceeds of sale and paid to the Respondent before calculation of the said shares.

1 This clause is for use where there is an endowment policy assigned collaterally with a mortgage, the sale of which is to be delayed, for example, under a *Mesher* or *Martin* order.

Settlement of property: simple order   C62

The Respondent do forthwith upon decree absolute settle upon _____ and _____ [*or* trustees, of whom one is to be appointed by the Petitioner and one by the Respondent] the property known as _____ upon trust for the Petitioner for life, remainder to such of the children of the family _____ and _____ as shall be living at her death and if more than one then in equal shares per stirpes and, in default of agreement as to the form of the deed of settlement, the matter to be referred to one of the conveyancing counsel of the court to settle [*or* the deed of settlement to be in the form of the draft attached marked "A"].

1 Matrimonial Causes Act 1973, s. 24.

2 The order cannot take effect until decree absolute (Matrimonial Causes Act 1973, s. 24(3)).

Variation of settlement: order extinguishing interest   C63

The [ante/post] nuptial settlement dated _____ and made between _____ and _____ be varied so as to extinguish the interest of the Respondent therein [*or* so as to settle all the interest of the Respondent therein on _____], [the settlement to be in the form of the draft deed attached marked "A"] [*or*, in default of agreement as to the form of the deed, the matter to be referred to conveyancing counsel of the court to settle].

1 Matrimonial Causes Act 1973, s. 24 (see B1–021).

2 The order cannot take effect until decree absolute (Matrimonial Causes Act 1973, s. 24(3)).

Transfer of tenancy   C64

Pursuant to Schedule 7 to the Family Law Act 1996 the interest of the Respondent in the dwelling house known as _____ by virtue of the [*set out details of the lease etc.*] be transferred to and vested in the Petitioner together with all the rights, privileges and appurtenances attaching to the Respondent's interest but subject to all covenants, obligations, liabilities and encumbrances under the said [lease *or as the case may be*].

1 Notice of the application for the proposed order should be served on the landlord in accordance with FPR 1991, r. 3.8(8). See *Crago v. Julian* [1992] 1 F.L.R. 478 and the article in *Family Law* at [1993] Fam. Law 8.

Rule of court   C65

The Minutes attached marked "A" be filed and made a rule of court.

1 *Practice Direction* [1972] 3 All E.R. 704 (extract) reads: "Where it is desired that terms of compromise should be filed and made a rule of court in lieu of being embodied in a court order, the same procedure [*i.e.* the lodging of a document setting out the agreed terms, signed by or on behalf of the parties] should be followed, and the terms, signed as above, must contain a specific provision that they are to be filed and made a rule of court."

2 This procedure is useful when it is desirable to record and seek the approval of the court to an agreement which cannot be made into a formal court order until decree nisi. It may, for example, be necessary where the parties wish to implement an agreement for the sale of a house before decree nisi.

3 The relevant paragraphs should be converted into a court order as soon as practicable.

4 The "Minutes" would typically be, or include, the draft consent order which the court will be asked to make on or after decree nisi.

Discharge of existing maintenance order on payment of lump sum   C66

Upon the [Respondent] undertaking and agreeing to pay to the Petitioner the sum of £____ on or before _____.

It is ordered by consent that:

1. The order herein dated _____ insofar as it relates to periodical payments to the Petitioner be varied so as to provide that the Respondent do continue to make periodical payments to the Petitioner at the rate therein referred to, namely _____, during joint lives until she shall remarry or until payment of the said sum of £____ whichever shall first occur.

2. Upon payment of the said sum of £____ the said order for periodical payments do stand discharged and the Petitioner's claim for periodical payments do stand dismissed and it is directed that the Petitioner shall not be entitled:
   (a) to make any further application in relation to the marriage for an order under section 23(1)(a) of the Matrimonial Causes Act 1973;
   (b) to apply under section 31 of the said Act for an extension of the term specified in paragraph 1; or

    (c) to apply on the death of the Respondent for an order under section 2 of the Inheritance (Provision for Family and Dependants) Act 1975.

1 This precedent envisages an agreed payment upon which maintenance will end. For a precedent based on the provisions of the Matrimonial Causes Act 1973, s. 31(7B), see C74.

2 As to the jurisdictional basis of the dismissal and direction in paragraph 2, see C43.

Dismissal of capital claims: order to be added at end of paragraph ordering lump sum, transfer of property etc.   C67

. . . and upon payment of the said lump sum [*or* such transfer *or as the case may be*] all the Petitioner's claims for secured periodical payments, [further or other] lump sum or sums and [further or other] property adjustment orders do stand dismissed and it is directed that the Petitioner shall not be entitled to make any further application in relation to the marriage for an order under section 23(1)(b) of the Matrimonial Causes Act 1973.

Dismissal of capital claims: order subject to implementation of agreement, compliance with undertakings etc.   C68

Subject to [*e.g.*, receipt by the Petitioner of her agreed share of the agreed proceeds of sale of the said former matrimonial home *or* compliance by the Respondent with his undertaking to ＿＿＿＿＿＿] [*add, if order to be taken out before decree absolute* and to the decree nisi herein being made absolute], all the Petitioner's claims for secured periodical payments, lump sum or sums and property adjustment orders do stand dismissed and it is directed that she shall not be entitled to make any further application in relation to the marriage for an order under section 23(1)(b) of the Matrimonial Causes Act 1973.

Inheritance Etc. Act: dismissal of one party's claims   C69

[Subject to the decree nisi herein being made absolute] the Petitioner shall not be entitled on the death of the Respondent to apply for an order under section 2 of the Inheritance (Provision for Family and Dependants) Act 1975.

1 Inheritance (Provision for Family and Dependants) Act 1975, s. 15 as amended by Matrimonial and Family Proceedings Act 1984, s. 8(1): "On the grant of a decree of divorce, a decree of nullity of marriage or a decree of judicial separation or at any time thereafter the court, if it considers it just to do so, may, on the application of either party to the marriage, order that the other party to the marriage shall not on the death of the applicant be entitled to apply for an order under section 2 of this Act."

2 It appears that some county courts require the words ". . . the court considering it just so to order" to be attached to an Inheritance Etc. Act dismissal. Whilst the court must of

course consider it just to make the order (see on this point *Whiting v. Whiting* [1988] 2 All E.R. 245), it is submitted that, given that the court's conclusion to this effect is a statutory requirement and therefore a *sine qua non* of the jurisdiction to make the order in the first place, the inclusion of the words referred to is unnecessary.

Inheritance Etc. Act: dismissal of both parties' claims   C70

[Subject to the decree nisi herein being made absolute] neither party shall be entitled upon the death of the other to apply for an order under section 2 of the Inheritance (Provision for Family and Dependants) Act 1975.

Clean break   C71

Subject to the decree nisi herein being made absolute [*or* subject to payment of the lump sum referred to in paragraph _____ *or as the case may be*]:

1. All the Petitioner's and the Respondent's [further or other] claims for periodical payments, secured periodical payments, lump sum or sums and property adjustment orders do stand dismissed and it is directed that neither shall be entitled to make any further application in relation to the marriage for an order under section 23(1)(a) or (b) of the Matrimonial Causes Act 1973.

2. Neither party shall be entitled on the death of the other to apply for an order under section 2 of the Inheritance (Provision for Family and Dependants) Act 1975.

1 The order should also contain a recital waiving claims under section 17 of the Married Women's Property Act (see C13).

Clean break: complete order where no other provisions are made   C72

Upon both parties acknowledging that neither has any outstanding claim against the other in respect of property including for the avoidance of doubt but not limited to claims under section 17 of the Married Women's Property Act 1882 as amended and extended

By consent it is ordered that:

[Subject to the decree nisi herein being made absolute] all the Petitioner's and Respondent's claims for periodical payments, secured periodical payments, lump sum or sums and property adjustment orders do stand dismissed and it is directed that neither shall be entitled to make any further application in relation to the marriage for an order under section 23(1)(a) or (b) of the Matrimonial Causes

Act 1973 or on the death of the other to apply for an order under section 2 of the Inheritance (Provision for Family and Dependants) Act 1975.

Clean break: order dismissing claims on judicial separation and consenting to a clean break on subsequent divorce   C73

Upon the parties agreeing and declaring as follows:

(a) The financial arrangements constituted by or recorded in this order are accepted by both of them in full and final satisfaction of all claims which each may have against the other or against the estate of the other under the Matrimonial Causes Act 1973, the Married Women's Property Act 1882 and the Inheritance (Provision for Family and Dependants) Act 1975 in each case as amended and extended, including all claims arising when the parties shall divorce.

(b) On _____, or on such earlier date as shall be agreed between the parties, the Respondent shall present a petition for divorce under section 1(2)(d) of the Matrimonial Causes Act 1973 or such statutory re-enactment thereof as shall then be in force or such statutory enactment as shall then be most similar in effect and both parties shall do all things necessary expeditiously to obtain a dissolution of their marriage in such proceedings.

(c) Both parties will consent (and hereby do consent) to an order being made in such proceedings reciting that neither of them has any outstanding property claim against the other and dismissing their respective claims against each other for periodical payments, secured periodical payments, lump sum or sums and property adjustment orders and their claims against each other's estates under section 2 of the Inheritance (Provision for Family and Dependants) Act 1975 and making such other provision as shall ensure that neither shall have any further claims against the other or the estate of the other.

(d) They have both signed Minutes of Order setting out the terms of the order referred to in the immediately preceding sub-paragraph and pro forma applications which said Minutes of Order and pro forma applications shall be retained by the Respondent's solicitors and the Petitioner hereby authorises the Respondent's solicitors to complete them as to the heading of the proceedings and to lodge them at court.

By consent it is ordered that:

1. All the claims of the Petitioner and Respondent for periodical payments, secured periodical payments, lump sum or sums and property adjustment orders do stand dismissed.

123

2.   Neither party shall be entitled on the death of the other to apply for an order under section 2 of the Inheritance (Provision for Family and Dependants) Act 1975.

1 A clean break cannot be effectively ordered on a judicial separation: the provisions of Matrimonial Causes Act 1973, s. 25A(3) and s. 28(1A) only apply on divorce or nullity decrees. An Inheritance Etc. Act dismissal can, however, be made on a decree of judicial separation: see section 15 of the Act set out at C69.

2 Whilst it would be unusual for a party who has obtained a full and proper financial settlement on judicial separation to seek further provision on divorce, the jurisdiction to permit her to do so remains. A judge might therefore refuse to accept the recitals on the grounds that they are an attempt to fetter the discretion of the court in the future.

Variation: lump sum in lieu of periodical payments   C74

The order herein dated _____ 20____ be varied and that:

(a)   The periodical payments order in favour of the Petitioner be discharged with effect from the date upon which the lump sum payable under the immediately following paragraph shall be paid [*or* with effect from _____] and with effect from that date the Petitioner's claim[s] for periodical payments [and secured periodical payments] do stand dismissed and it is directed that she shall not be entitled to make any further application in relation to the marriage for an order under section 23(1)(a) or (b) of the Matrimonial Causes Act 1973.

(b)   Pursuant to section 31(7B) of the Matrimonial Causes Act 1973, the Respondent do on or before _____ 20____ pay to the Petitioner a lump sum of £____.

(c)   Pursuant to section 28(1A) of the Matrimonial Causes Act 1973, the Petitioner shall not be entitled to apply for an extension of the term specified in paragraph (a) above or to apply on the death of the Respondent for an order under section 2 of the Inheritance (Provision for Family and Dependants) Act 1975.

1 Matrimonial Causes Act 1973, s. 31(7B) inserted by paragraph 16(7) of Schedule 8 to the Family Law Act 1996.

2 The amendment is retrospective; paragraph 6(2) of Schedule 9 to the Family Law Act 1996 provides: "Subsections (7) to (7F) of [section 31] also have effect as amended by this Act in relation to any order made before the coming into force of the amendments."

3 Although as a general rule it is unnecessary to state the statutory provision under which an order of the court is made, this may be one of those cases where it is desirable. As to the jurisdictional basis of the dismissal and direction in paragraph (a) see C43.

Variation: periodical payments   C75

The order herein dated _____ 20____ (insofar as it relates to period-ical payments to the Petitioner) be varied and that:

(a) The Respondent do make or cause to be made to the Petitioner with effect from _____ during joint lives until she shall remarry or further order periodical payments at the rate of £____ a year payable monthly [in advance];

(b) The Respondent be released from his undertaking to _____.

(c) The arrears accrued up to _____ 20____ be remitted.

1 Matrimonial Causes Act 1973, s. 31(1), (2) and (2A).

Costs: orders on interlocutory hearings (various)   C76

(a) Costs in the application.

(b) Costs in the inquiry.

(c) Petitioner's costs in the application [or inquiry].

(d) Costs reserved to [the district judge hearing the ancillary relief applica-tion].

1 The effects of the foregoing orders are, respectively, as follows:

(a) The party who is awarded costs on the substantive hearing will get the costs of the interlocutory hearing.

(b) The same as (a) where more than one application is being heard at the same time.

(c) The Petitioner will get her costs if she is awarded costs on the substantive hearing, but will not have to pay the Respondent's costs if she fails to do so.

(d) The costs will be decided at a later hearing. The old rule about costs reserved in family proceedings has been reversed; if no specific order for the reserved costs is made at the later hearing, they will be costs in the application (CPR 48PD-004).

2 Costs in family proceedings are now subject to rr. 43, 44 (except rr. 44.9 to 44.12), 47 and 48 of the Civil Procedure Rules 1998.

Costs: no order   C77

There be no order as to costs [save Legal Aid assessment pursuant to regulation 107A of the Civil Legal Aid (General) Regulations 1989 of the Petitioner's costs] [the Petitioner undertaking not to seek to enforce the order for costs made on _____].

Costs: agreed contribution C78

The Respondent do [on or before _____] pay the Petitioner's costs in the agreed sum of £_____ including VAT and disbursements.

Costs: order with exclusions C79

The Respondent do pay the Petitioner's costs including the costs of negotiations and implementation [but excluding the fees of Messrs _____ and the costs of the Petitioner's solicitors incurred in connection with instructing them and generally in connection with the work undertaken by them] on the [standard/ indemnity] basis to be assessed if not agreed.

Costs: orders against legally aided party (various) C80

- (a) The Petitioner do pay the Respondent's costs, such costs not to be enforced without leave of the court.
- (b) The determination of the amount of the [*assisted person*]'s liability for costs be adjourned to _____.
- (c) The Petitioner do pay the Respondent's costs, such costs to be paid on or before _____.
- (d) Respondent's costs, Petitioner's liability assessed at nil.

1 The effects of the foregoing orders are, respectively, as follows:
- (a) The Respondent must apply to the court subsequently for enforcement. Such an order should not be made unless there are reasonable prospects of a successful enforcement (*Parr v. Smith* [1996] 1 F.L.R 490).
- (b) The determination of an assisted party's liability for costs may be adjourned for such time and to such place as the court thinks fit (Civil Legal Aid (General) Regulations 1989, reg. 129(a)).
- (c) The court may suspend the time for payment by an assisted party until a fixed date or indefinitely (Civil Legal Aid (General) Regulations 1989, reg. 129(b)).
- (d) This applies where the Respondent is entitled to his costs, but cannot recover them from the legally aided Petitioner because of s. 17 of the Legal Aid Act 1988 or s. 11 of the Access to Justice Act 1999. The Respondent may then apply for an order against the Legal Services Commission.

Costs: postponement of legal aid charge C81

It is certified for the purpose of the Civil Legal Aid (General) Regulations 1989 [that the lump sum of _____ has been ordered to be paid to enable the

Petitioner to purchase a home for herself (or her dependants)] [that the property _____ has been [preserved/recovered] for the Petitioner for use as a home for herself (or her dependants)].

1 This follows the wording suggested in the Senior District Judge's *Practice Direction* of August 19, 1991 [1991] 2 F.L.R. 384.

Notes on drafting consent orders

C82

1   Terms which come within the courts' statutory powers, for example, under sections 23 and 24 of the 1973 Act, should be expressed to be orders. All other terms should be undertakings or agreements recited in the preamble to the order.

2   The order should make clear precisely what claims or potential claims are to be dismissed. Almost all settlements reached on divorce are intended to be in satisfaction of the parties' capital claims and the order should expressly dismiss the claims for lump sum or sums and property adjustment orders. If capital claims are to include secured periodical payments, as arguably they should, there must be a dismissal and a direction that no further applications may be made under section 23(1)(b) of the 1973 Act.

3   The order should be clear as to when the dismissals are to take effect. Typically they would take effect on compliance with capital orders and undertakings intended to have immediate effect. It is undesirable for dismissals to take effect on compliance with undertakings of a continuing nature, for such undertakings may not be fulfilled for many years and may be subject to release on a subsequent variation.

4   There must be a time limit within which an order or undertaking is to be complied with. Ordinarily "forthwith" will be adequate, but there will always be cases where the prospect of enforcement, particularly enforcement abroad, dictates that precise dates should be stipulated.

5   Orders of a capital nature cannot be made until decree nisi and cannot come into effect until decree absolute and orders should be drafted so that the time for compliance does not offend the latter rule. Where the approval of the court is sought to financial arrangements which are to be effected before decree, consideration should be given to making the agreement a Rule of Court (see precedent C65).

6   The court will not accept undertakings which fetter its discretion in the future, for example, an undertaking not to apply to vary a maintenance order.

7   Where a party has agreed to set up a trust, give a covenant etc., the documents should whenever possible be agreed before the order is made.

CHINA BASICS SERIES

CHINA TOURISM

Exploring a Dreamland

Author: Li Hairui   Translator: Chen Gengtao

August, 1998

CHINA INTERCONTINENTAL PRESS

中国基本情况丛书

顾　　问　李　冰　赵少华

主　　编　金　晖

编　　委　宋坚之(执行)　吴　伟

编　　辑　杨季明　冯凌宇　潘仙英

装帧设计　宁成春(特约)　田　林

本册编辑　张　宏

图书在版编目(CIP)数据

中国旅游:英文/李海瑞著. – 北京:五洲传播出版社,1998.5
(中国基本情况丛书)

ISBN 7 – 80113 – 350 – 1

Ⅰ.中… Ⅱ.李… Ⅲ.旅游业 – 概况 – 中国 – 英文　Ⅳ.F592

中国版本图书馆 CIP 数据核字(98)第 08374 号

五洲传播出版社　　出版发行

北京北三环中路 31 号　　邮政编码 100088

HTTP://WWW.CHINA.ORG.CN/CICC

*

利丰雅高制作(深圳)有限公司制版印刷

1998 年 8 月第 1 版第 1 次印刷

889 × 1194 毫米　32 开　5.25 印张　55 千字

ISBN 7 – 80113 – 350 – 1 /F·25

(004500)

Table Of Contents

INTRODUCTION

At a time when the world is often referred to as the "global village," people in the west hemisphere often regard going to China as a "dream," one that is far away and mysterious. Even in the Arab world which, like China, is located in Asia, a folk saying goes: "Be it as far away as China, it is worth going for the sake of seeking knowledge."

I once met a 94-year-old lady from Georgia of the United States at the Badaling section of the Great Wall. When she was four years old, she told

me, her grandmother said to her that there was a country in a faraway place called China, where there is an ancient, long wall called the Great Wall. This had been alive in her mind for 90 years, a long, inescapable dream, she said. "At long last," she said with a smile, "my dream has come true."

In Bremen, Germany, I knew a college-educated girl Doris. She and her mother had been to China, going there via the ancient Silk Road: entering the Chinese region of Xinjiang from Tajikstan and continuing the journey eastward by riding on freight trucks, camels and trains. Along the way, they toured many places and saw

The Hukou Waterfall on the Yellow River

lifestyles and folk customs. Their trip to Beijing took two months. Back in Germany, they wrote a 300 - page book about the trip. "This is a most marvelous experience for me," she said.

Mr. Iwada, a Japanese, has visited China many times. He has been to Beijing, Nanjing, Hangzhou, Xi'an, Dunhuang, Luoyang and Kaifeng. Sites that attracted him include palaces, gardens, ancient tombs and old - fashioned residential houses. He would read carefully Chinese characters engraved on stone tablets. "Japanese culture has its roots

The Great Wall, an ancient defensive work running across northern China

in China," he said. "Travels in China are a textbook for me."

Since the late 1970s, China has opened its doors to the rest of the world, giving rise to a new industry — tourism. For people in the rest of the world, China is no longer far away, although some of its areas have remained mysterious to outsiders.

Peoples in different parts of the world view China from different perspectives. But they have a common wish: to see China with their own eyes if there is an opportunity to do so.

LOOKING FOR
SITES OF ANCIENT CHINA

China is home to one of the world's four ancient civilizations. Latest archaeological data show that primitive pictographic characters used by ancient Chinese date back 7,000 years, and that areas along the Yangtze as well as the Yellow River are the cradle of Chinese civilization. In the Yangtze encatchment area, archaeologists have recently found rice seeds and primitive tools for rice cultivation that date back 7,000 years.

The 7,000 – year Chinese civilization is comparable with ancient Egyptian, Babylonian and Indian civilizations. In some areas, the Chinese civilization predated its peers. Places of historical interest and cultural relics can be found everywhere in the country. Those officially listed alone number more than 5,000.

The most famous is naturally the Great Wall. With a total length of 6,350 km, it extends across northern China, from the Shanhaiguan Pass on the Bohai Sea in the east to the Jiayu Pass in Gansu province in the west. If sections of the Great Wall built by all dynastic rulers in more than 2,000 years between the 7th century B.C. and the 16th century A.D. were "linked" together, the total length would be more than 50,000 km, long enough to run around the earth at the equator and to spare. It is no wonder that the Americans who landed on the moon reportedly saw clearly the outline of the Great Wall with naked eyes when they looked back at their home planet.

The Great Wall to the Chinese nation is what the pyramids are to Egypt. It is a symbol of the country. "He who has not climbed up the Great Wall is no hero," a Chinese saying goes. For the international traveler, a visit to Egypt without

Visiting China
for the first time

The Forbidden City in Beijing – the bastion of imperial rule in the Ming and Qing dynasties. It was built in 1406 and repeatedly renovated later.

seeing at least one of the pyramids can hardly be regarded as a true visit to the country, nor can a visit to China without climbing the Great Wall be regarded as a true China visit.

The Palace Museum in the heart of the city, also called "the Forbidden City," is a cluster of halls and palaces for use by ancient rulers of China. It is enclosed by a wall forming a rectangular enclosure. The wall is ten meters high and measures 760 meters from east to west and 960 meters from north to south. The enclosure covers an area of more than 720,000 square meters. Inside the enclosure are 999.5 rooms — the biggest royal palace in the world.

For more than 500 years, 24 emperors of the

Ming and Qing dynasties lived in this Forbidden City. Inside are imposing palaces and halls, all elaborately decorated. On a clear day, viewed from above, the complex presents a vast expanse of glittering yellow — the color of glazed tiles covering the roof tops of all buildings there. At each corner of the city is a multi - eaved tower. And the City is surrounded by a moat.

A short distance north of the Tiananmen Gate is the Wumen Gate, the main entrance to the Forbidden City. The cluster of halls and palaces in the southern part of the City is where emperors handled state affairs, gave audiences to officials and received foreign envoys. The inner part of the City consists of adjoining courtyard houses–living quarters for the queen and the emperor's numerous concubines. Innermost is a royal garden with winding paths, tiny pavilions and grotesque rockery.

Today, in each hall or room are displayed articles once used by emperors and their families. Some halls are devoted to the display of treasures of various dynasties. With its ancient buildings and vast amounts of treasures on display inside, the Forbidden City makes a truly great museum.

This vast palatial complex enclosed by a high crimson wall, for hundreds of years, was where political intrigues were plotted and battles for succession fought. "The Last Emperor," an Oscar

- winning movie, was shot inside the Forbidden City and is based on life lived by its inhabitants.

Henry Kissinger, a former secretary of state of the United States, who has visited China many times, maintains that the Temple of Heaven in Beijing is a gem of classic Chinese architecture and has the highest value.

The Temple of Heaven is where emperors offered sacrifices to Heaven. It was built more than 500 years ago. Each Chinese emperor called himself "the Son of Heaven" and presided over annual sacrificial ceremonies in person. The Temple of Heaven covers an area twice as big as that of the Forbidden City. It is actually a royal garden with large tracts of wooded land but few buildings. The central building in the garden is the Hall of Prayer for Good Harvests, for which Dr. Kissinger is all admiration. He recalled that when he first saw the Hall, he was too awe - stricken to have any words for its beauty. The Hall, round in shape, is 38 meters tall and 30 meters across. It has a white round base, blue tiles, red columns and a gold -plated top. Architecturally, its uniqueness lies in its three overlapping roofs supported by 28 huge wood beams and a complex array of inter - connected wood structures. It is a masterpiece typical of Chinese wooden architecture.

Another attraction of the Temple of Heaven is the Echo Wall. Two people standing out of ear-

Listening to echoes from the Echo Wall in the Temple of Heaven

The Hall of Prayer for Good Harvests. The hall is inside the 270-hectare Temple of Heaven in Beijing.

shot at any point along the wall can hear each other talking. This is an ingenious use of acoustics by the Chinese 500 years ago.

There are in China many other ancient buildings with unique characteristics. The Hanging Temple in a ravine in Shanxi province is an example. The temple, built 1,500 years ago, hangs virtually from a perpendicular cliff, its base being hewn out of rock. The three – storied temple is of a wooden structure, and its top is 50 meters above the ground. An ordinary temple in China would identify itself with a particular religious sect, but this is not the way with the Hanging Temple. Worshipped simultaneously in the temple are Sakyamuni, the founder of Buddhism, Laozi, the founder of Taoism, and Confucius, the founder of Confucianism.

The most mystic ancient building in China may

be the Potala Palace in Tibet built in the seventh century. Located on a hill in the northwestern part of Lhasa, the regional capital of Tibet, the Potala is the biggest castle – like building and the highest in altitude in the world. Built of granite, the Potala covers 41 hectares of land and has 13 stories with a total of 1,000 rooms. All the Dalai Lamas lived and officiated in the palace. The Dalai Lama's bedroom is at the top of the palace and exposed to the sun all day long, hence it is called the Sunlight Hall. The stupa where the remains

of past Dalai Lamas are kept is also placed in the palace. The palace's chanting rooms, Buddhist statues, sculptures and murals as well as a huge amount of Buddhist classics and treasures kept inside have very high historical and cultural values. In recent years, the Chinese government has spent 53 million yuan repairing and renovating the Potala and restored it to its former grandeur.

In contrast to architectural behemoths are small, exquisite gardens of the classic Suzhou style. The city of Suzhou, which lies a short dis-

A garden in Suzhou, Jiangsu Province

tance to the west of Shanghai, has a concentration of such gardens including Cang Lang Ting, Shi Zi Lin, Wan Shi Yuan and Liu Yuan. They embody the gardening techniques of the Song, Yuan, Ming and Qing dynasties. Since most of them were scholars' private residences, they are small in size. With fancy buildings and pavilions that are separated by rockery, flowers and trees but linked by winding paths, these gardens are re – creations of nature in a limited space.

Ancient residential houses in Shexian county in Anhui province's Huizhou prefecture are of another style. In the past, when Huizhou businessmen made fortunes by engaging in trade away from home, they would buy land and build huge residences back home. In the county are close to 100 residences of this kind built 400 – 500 years

Residential houses in southern Anhui's Yixian County dating back to Ming and Qing periods.

ago during the Ming Dynasty. These residences feature tall and closed anti – fire walls, elaborately – designed fronts, square courtyards, carved wooden doors, windows and railings, and noisy wooden stairs. These reflect the very subtle mentality of the Huizhou businessmen: they loved to enjoy a life of extravagance but would not like their lifestyle to be revealed.

Farther back in history, in very ancient times, people's residences were simple and primitive. The Banpo Village on the outskirts of Xi'an is the site of a matriarchal clan community that existed 6,000 years ago in the Yellow River valley. Among the ruins of 45 primitive houses are those built half underground and those built on the ground with wooden support. The houses are either round or square in shape, and all face south. At

The Xuankong Temple on Mount Hengshan in Shanxi Province. "Xuankong" means "suspended in mid-air" in Chinese.

16 CHINA TOURISM – Exploring A Dreamland

The Potala Palace in Lhasa, the capital of the Tibet Autonomous Region

the center of each house is a pit for cooking. The houses were built of clay, grass and wood. Around the houses are cellars for storing things, kilns for making earthen ware, and graves.

Dujiangyan near Chengdu, Sichuan, built more than 2,200 years ago, is the earliest big irrigation project in the world. The marvel is the project's enduring vitality: it is still operating normally today in its original form. The project consists in dividing the Minjiang river into two, one for flood release and the other for irrigation/navigation. Today, the project irrigates 600,000 hectares of farmland. Dujiangyan with two nearby temples and a suspension bridge is now a tourist attrac-

Dujiangyan - an ancient irrigation project in Sichuan Province, southwest China, which is still in use today.

tion.

But two cities as ancient as the irrigation project have fared badly. Located near Turpan in the central Asian region of Xinjiang, the ancient cities of Gaochang and Jiaohe flourished for some 1,000 years before going into oblivion. Today, although the sites consists mainly of crumbled walls of ochre clay, many things are still discernible thanks to the dry climate of the area: bases of city walls, streets, temples, Buddhist pagodas, residential houses, wells, official buildings, workshops and markets. Standing amid the ruins and imagining the cities' once bustling life, visitors cannot but feel overcome temporarily by the vicissitudes of life.

Recent years have seen the building of imitation ancient Chinese cities in some countries and regions in the world. This reflects their interest in China. Such imitation cities are usually patterned after Xi'an, capital of the Tang Dynasty (618 – 907), Kaifeng, capital of the Northern Song Dynasty (960 – 1127), or Nanjing, capital of the Ming Dynasty (1368 – 1644). The Ming court moved to present – day Beijing after ruling in Nanjing for more than 50 years). These (real) ancient Chinese cities serve as vivid history books to Chinese and foreign visitors alike. In all of them, the ancient city walls are still there, with some sections repaired and renovated strictly according to their original designs. Some

Ruins of an ancient city on the Silk Road. Gaochang, a once prosperous city, lies in today's Xinjiang, a Chinese autonomous region in central Asia.

streets in these cities have regained their original, historical look.

In the 1970s, near the tomb of the first emperor of a unified China not far from the city of Xi'an, was discovered a huge terra – cotta army that had been buried underground for 22 centuries. The discovery caught the attention of the world, and the clay army was reputed to be the Eighth Wonder of the World. Evidently the Qin

emperor, when he was alive, would like to keep a huge army in afterlife. As a result, near his mausoleum were buried thousands of life – size, painted terra – cotta soldiers and horses and various kinds of weapons actually used in wars at the time. Later, archaeologists also found a bronze chariot and a cave resembling the headquarters of an army at times of war. Altogether, close to 10,000 articles were unearthed. The terra – cotta soldiers

Pit with terra-cotta soldiers and horses, a burial project for Emperor Qin Shi Huang (who reigned 221B.C.-209B.C.). A total of about 8,000 life-size earthen soldiers and horses have been unearthed from the pit.

The Mogao Caves in Dunhuang, Gansu Province, are known as a treasurehouse of Buddhist art. Picture shows Buddhist statues and murals inside one of the caves there.

and horses, arranged in battle formations, seem to form a strong, spirited army ready for battle.

China's ancient grotto art, or stone carving, is exquisite. Most artistic works have Buddhism as their theme and all sites have a history of more than 1,000 years. Among the best – known sites are the Yungang Grottoes near Datong, Shanxi province; the Longmen Grottoes near Luoyang, Henan province; grottoes at Mount Maijishan near Tianshui, Gansu province; and stone carvings in Dazu county, Sichuan province. The Buddha Statue near the city of Leshan, Sichuan province, which is 71 meters tall and has a shoulder width of 28 meters, was created in the Tang Dynasty (about 1,000 years ago) and is the world's biggest stone statue of the Buddha. It took workmen 90 years to hew the statue out of a natural

The stone Buddha in Leshan, Sichuan Province. The biggest of its kind in the world, the statue has been included on the World Natural and Cultural Dual Heritage List by the UN Educational, Scientific and Cultural Organization.

stone slope. The imposing stone Buddha faces a vast expanse of water where three rivers meet.

Of the stone grottoes, the most famous is the Mugao Grottoes at Dunhuang, Gansu province, which has long been known as "a treasurehouse of oriental art." At Mugao, about 1,000 grottoes containing Buddhism – related art works are spread over a 1,600 – meter – long cliff, and they were hewn out of the cliff over a millennium starting from 366 A.D. At a time when the ancient Silk Road served as a major link for economic and cultural exchanges between the east and west, businessmen, officials and ordinary people traveling along the Road needed places of worship to pray for safety. They came to Dunhuang to hew grottoes out of cliffs, create Buddhist statues and worship. That is how the Mugao Grottoes came into being. Up to now, 492 grottoes built over ten

A tour-oriented caravan of camels on the Silk Road

Sketch Map for
Silk Road Tours

dynasties have been well preserved, and they contain more than 45,000 square meters of murals and more than 2,000 color statues.

Aside from Buddhist themes, murals in the Mugao Grottoes depict customs, lifestyles and cultural activities in different dynasties. Among the most intriguing are dance girls playing pipa and nude goddesses traveling in space. The grottoes contain vast amounts of valuable data and images for studying China's and even the Orient's ancient politics, economy, military affairs and culture. In fact, the study of the grottoes has evolved into a special branch of learning called Dunhuang Xue in Chinese, or Dunhuangology in English.

While Xi'an is the starting point of the ancient Silk Road, Dunhuang is a communications hub on the road. From Dunhuang, the Silk Road forks into three routes westward into Xinjiang. For more than 2,000 years, the Silk Road served as an international trade route. Today, it is a flourishing tour route, its attraction lying chiefly in a great number of sites of historical interest that are strewn alongside it: ancient cities, ancient temples, ancient pagodas, ancient tombs, ancient stone carvings and ancient caves.

Dunhuang's Mugao Grottoes, together with the Great Wall, the Forbidden City, the Mausoleum of Emperor Qin Shihuang and the Potala Palace, have been included on the World Cultural Heritage List by the UN Educational, Scientific and Cultural Organization.

It has been suggested that, for a foreign visitor to see the best of China in different historical periods, he or she should go to Xi'an to see China of 2,000 years ago, to Beijing 1,000 years ago, and to Shanghai 100 years ago. Shanghai epitomizes modern China and has many sites of historical interest that have been left behind in the past century. Among them are a site of the Taiping Heavenly Kingdom, a peasant uprising sweeping almost half of China in the 19th century, foreign – style buildings that date to the early years of Shanghai as a port of foreign trade, residences of such well – known figures as Dr. Sun Yat – sen, Soong Chingling and Lu Xun, and the site of the founding of the Communist Party of China. Nowadays, at the forefront of reform and opening to the rest of the world, Shanghai is changing fast. It is well worth while to go there and see how it has changed. Recommended sites include the two giant bridges spanning the Huangpu, the "Oriental Pearl" TV tower, the new underground railway, elevated highways, the newly – expanded Bund, the People's Square, the Yuyuan Market in the Old City, and high – rise buildings of different styles that come up everywhere in the crowded city. The atmosphere of Shanghai as a of tourists, domestic and foreign.

The Nanpu Bridge
in Shanghai

ENTERING PICTURES OF MOUNTAINS AND WATERS

A tour in many parts of China often seems to enter a landscape painting.

Guilin is a place where a visitor feels being in a landscape painting. Hills here do not form undulating ranges. Rather, they are scattered here and there, independent of one another. Shaped like a cone or a cylinder, they resemble giant stalagmites growing abruptly out of the earth. Such terrain has resulted from long erosion by water of limestone structures. Naturally, Guilin abounds in karst grottoes of all conceivable shapes and sizes. Stalagmites, stalactites and helictites make each grotto a wondrous world.

The Guilin area is crisscrossed by rivers and dotted with lakes. Steep green peaks set amid a watery world make enchanting pictures. The city of Guilin itself is built in between hills and alongside rivers. Guilin is known as "a city within a landscape, with also landscapes within the city."

A good way to enjoy Guilin scenery is to tour the Lijiang River by boat. The 83 – km section of the Lijiang from Guilin to Yangshuo, flowing amid, and reflecting, green peaks, presents scenes of natural beauty and an idyllic life at every turn. Between hills on both sides of the river are farm-houses, fishermen's cottages, green farmland, woods and groves of bamboo. On the water are bamboo rafts, fishermen, water buffaloes and cowherd playing with water. At night, on bamboo rafts faintly lighted with kerosene lamps sit black cormorants which would now and then plunge into the water and come up with fish in their beaks. The fisherman would catch hold of the fish and put them into a basket. To see how cormo-rants catch fish is a popular item of night tour on the Lijiang River.

Guilin scenery

"Guilin's scenic beauty has no rival in the world" has been a popular perception for thousands of years in China. A Chinese poet once said that he would be a Guilin resident rather than an immortal in heaven. Richard Nixon, a former president of the United States, said that no natural beauty elsewhere in the world is comparable with Guilin's. Beautiful scenery can be found everywhere in the world. Guilin's "no rival" reputation is due mainly to the uniqueness of its landscape and the marvelous combination of its abrupt peaks and rivers. In scenic beauty, in fact, Guilin has many rivals in China, though each has its own characteristics.

The Three Gorges section of the Yangtze River is a natural wonder resulting from the hand of nature. It runs 193 km, from Bai Di Cheng — a shrine on top of a riverside hill dedicated to a king — in Fengjie County, Chongqing Municipality, to Nanjin Pass in Yichang City, Hubei Province. The river at this section, squeezed and darkened by towering mountains on both sides, is a rushing torrent. Downstream from west to east

Sketch Map for
Three Gorges Tours

Da Ning River 大宁河
Baidi Shrine 白帝城
Qu Tang Gol. 瞿塘峡
巫山 Wushan
巫峡 Wu Gorge
Goddess Peak 神女峰
奉节 Fengjie
巴东 Badong
秭归 Zigui
香溪 Xiangxi
Zhaojun's Hometown
西陵峡 Xiling Gorge
湖北 Hubei
三斗坪 Sandou Isle
三游洞 Sanyou Cave
葛洲坝 Gezhou Dam
宜昌 Yichang

are the Qutang Gorge, the Wuxia Gorge and the Xiling Gorge. There is in this area another natural wonder called the Lesser Three Gorges, which actually is a section of the Daning River that empties into the Three Gorges of the Yangtze. A sightseer riding a boat on the section is greeted by green mountain slopes, grotesque peaks and waterfalls. River water is clear and, at places, torrential. No wonder the Lesser Three Gorges has become a popular tourist destination.

A tour of the Three Gorges of the Yangtze by ship brings the traveler to numerous sites of historical interest along the way, including Bai Di Cheng, the Qu Yuan Temple (Qu Yuan was an ancient poet) and the hometown of Lady Wang Zhaojun (who married the leader of a minority ethnic group in ancient China). Tourists will also find it interesting to observe the customs and

The Yangtze is China's longest river and one of the world's longest rivers. Its Three Gorges section is a prime tourist destination.

simple lifestyle of people living in towns and villages along this section of the river.

The Three Gorges Hydroelectric Project now under construction gives domestic and overseas travel agents an excuse to launch promotional campaigns for "Farewell Tours" along the Three Gorges. Actually, when the Yangtze is dammed, creating a huge man – made lake upstream, there will be additions to, as well as reductions of, scenic sights along the Three Gorges area. Some hidden reefs will be submerged far deeper than they are today. This might take away some thrill from travel along this section of the Yangtze but will make it much safer. Buildings of historical inter-

est and cultural relics will be relocated to higher ground, while stone carvings which cannot be moved will be preserved in a museum to be built on the site under water. After the dam is built, numerous streams, which are now too shallow for navigation, will swell up enormously to become so many "Lesser Three Gorges," offering tourists ship rides on their placid surface and views of spectacular mountains on all sides. By then, the Three Gorges Reservoir area will have a tour network consisting of crisscrossing water routes.

Jiuzhaigou, or Nine - Stockade Gully, located amid tall mountains in northern Sichuan province, was not known until the mid - 1960s when lum-

Jiuzhaigou, or Nine-Stockade Gully, in northwestern Sichuan Province

berjacks constructing a highway discovered its existence in a pristine state. Its fame has since spread far and wide.

The beauty of Jiuzhaigou is a simple, pure beauty. It is everywhere, in the crystal blue sky, in pure white clouds, in clear, transparent water and in mountain slopes that seem to drip with greenness. Lakes in the area, big and small, assume different hues with the change of sunlight and the change of seasons, adding a magic flavor to Jiuzhaigou's beauty.

Jiuzhaigou, which has an area of 720 square kilometers, is located at where the Sichuan Basin joins the Qinghai – Tibet Plateau. It is an area characterized by the widest range of changes in terrain. Within the area are tall mountains, deep ravines, forests, grass – covered slopes, lakes, waterfalls, streams and gullies, all in a pristine state. Some woods grow right on gurgling streams. In the woods, above the water, winding paths made of wooden planks have been built. Tourists explore the woods and streams by walking on and following the paths. All the while, water flows under their feet. Above a waterfall is a giant, slightly – sloping stone slab called Zhenzhutan, or the Pearl Terrace. Standing on the slab, tourists can feel water flowing past their feet and plunging down below as the waterfall.

Jiuzhaigou is named after the nine stockade vil-

lages that are spread along the gou, or gully. In
the quiet gully are occasionally seen Tibetan –
style wooden houses and small wooden bridges
and water – driven mills on streams. It is a land
of peace and quiet beauty, away from the turmoil
of the world.

Jiuzhaigou lies more than 400 km to the northwest of Chengdu, the provincial capital of Sichuan.
Its tour area is located at elevations of 1,980 – 3,100
meters above the sea level. With an average temperature of 2.5 degrees Celsius in January, the cold-
est month, and an average temperature of 17 degrees Celsius in July, the hottest month, Jiuzhaigou
is fit for sightseeing all the year round. In 1992, the
scenic area was listed as a World Natural Heritage

site by the United Nations.

The group of waterfalls, at Huangguoshu in southwest China's Guizhou province, is among the most spectacular sights in China. The Huangguoshu tourist area consists of 18 above – ground and four underground waterfalls, stone forests and karst caves, which are spread around in a 200 – square – km area. It is never hot here. At the turn of spring and summer, when rivers swell with rain, splashing waterfalls make wonderful sights. The best – known waterfall is the Huangguoshu, which is 81 meters wide and 71 meters high. The roar of the waterfall can be heard five km away, and a perpetual mist hangs over the waterfall. In the dry season, the waterfall divides into four and becomes slightly tamer.

Viewed from whatever angle — from above, down under, close at hand or afar, the Huangguoshu Waterfall has a unique beauty. The most novel way to see the waterfall is perhaps to get into a cave behind the waterfall and view the plunging curtain of water from there.

There are many famous mountains in China. The Chinese in ancient times regarded the following five as sacred mountains: Taishan (called East Mountain, in Shandong), Huashan (West Mountain, in Shaanxi), Hengshan (South Mountain, in Hunan), Hengshan (North Mountain, in Shanxi) and Songshan (Central Mountain, in

The Welcoming Pine–a representative scene on Mount Huangshan

Mount Huangshan in Anhui Province, regarded as being the most beautiful and awe-
inspiring among China's famous mountains

Henan). Xu Xiake, a well – known geographer active in the Ming period, regarded the five mountains as being representative of mountains in China, commenting, "No mountain would interest those who have returned from a trip to the Five Mountains." On the other hand, however, he regarded Mount Huangshan as the best of all mountains, commenting, "None of the Five Mountains would interest those who have returned from a trip to Mount Huangshan."

Mount Huangshan is indeed worthy of the

reputation. It has almost all the characteristics of other famous mountains, such as the imposing grandeur of Mount Taishan, the precipitousness of Mount Huashan, the mist of Mount Hengshan, the waterfalls of Mount Lushan (in Jiangxi), the coolness of Mount Emei (in Sichuan), and the grotesque stones of Mount Yantang (in Zhejiang). Mount Huangshan has a total of 72 peaks, big and small, with the highest towering more than 1,800 meters above the sea level. Strange in shape and precipitous, the peaks present different scenery

Peaks of the Tianzi Mountain in the Wulingyuan scenic area in Hunan province

with the change of seasons. Mount Huangshan is known for four things: strange – shaped pine trees, grotesque stones, a sea of clouds, and hot springs. Ancient pines growing on perpendicular cliffs assume all kinds of shapes, giving rise to the saying: "No cliff is free of pine trees, and no pine tree is conventional in shape." Stones of all shapes are strewn all over the mountain. Mist that often envelopes the whole mountain or hangs halfway up gives tourists the impression that they are in the ninth heaven. Water of the hot springs here is so clear that it is fit for drinking as well as bathing. It is often observed that mist floats up and down quickly along ridges, revealing or hiding peaks that stand close by or at a distance. Mount Huangshan has given inspiration to many painters. Liu Haisu, a renowned painter who lived up to 100 years, climbed up Mount Huangshan more than ten times in his lifetime for such inspiration.

Mount Huangshan, together with Mount Taishan, has been included on the UNESCO's World Natural and Cultural Heritage List.

Generally speaking, to tour a mountain means to climb up that mountain. But the Wuyi Mountain in Fujian province is an exception. Here, rather than climb uphill, tourists leisurely see sights of the mountain by cruising on water.

Wuyi consists of numerous low hills, the tallest of them measuring no more than 500 meters above the sea level. Usually, a single giant stone makes a peak characterized by steep slopes and a flat top. Almost every peak here is surrounded by water, and streams follow the run of the peaks in taking twists and turns. Bamboo rafts offering rides to tourists are easily available. Each raft can accommodate three people and is maneuvered by

Rafting under shadows of Mount Wuyi in Fujian Province

a boatman. Tourists sit comfortably in bamboo chairs on the raft, which flows quietly on the clear Jiuqu River, round one peak after another. Water lightly laps the bamboo raft, and the green mountains on both sides recede slowly. The tourists seem to have entered a landscape painting.

Wulingyuan in Hunan province, covering 264 square km, is another unique scenic area. It consists of the Zhangjiajie State Forest Park, the Suoxi Valley and a scenic mountainous area called Tianzishan. Owing to erosion by water, the 13 - square - km Zhangjiajie State Forest Park is shaped like a basin with its peripheries ringed by thousands of perpendicular cliffs and peaks, whose layers of red sandrock are clearly discernible. Viewed from a distance, the cliffs and peaks seem to have been formed of layers of huge rocks

placed one on another. Everywhere in the area
are ancient trees and tracts of forests. In fact,
tree coverage here reaches 97.7 percent. With an
annual mean temperature of 16 degrees Celsius,
warm winters and cool summers, Zhangjiajie is
fit for tours all the year round.

Zhangjiajie is known as "nature's labyrinth"
where "each step takes one into a whole new
world of breathtaking beauty." And a beauty that
is pristine and wild. Climbing to the top of
Huangshizhai, tourists command a spectacular
view of peaks around, and they can also walk
slowly along gurgling streams flanked by cliffs,
amid a profound quietness.

Wulingyuan and Jiuzhaigou have been included
in the World's Natural and Cultural Heritage List
by UNESCO.

Another tour destination with a mystic flavor is Shennongjia, a 3,000 - square - km mountainous area in northwestern Hubei province. The area boasts vast tracts of virgin forests, exotic plants and rare animals. For many years, sightings of the "Wild Man" in the area have been reported but never confirmed. Shennongjia is a good place for ecology tours.

One of the most time - honored scenic areas in China is the West Lake in Hangzhou, Zhejiang province, east China, which has long been known as "paradise on earth" since ancient times. The

Winter releases the magic hand of riming in northeast China

West Lake is surrounded by mountains on three sides and borders the city of Hangzhou on the other side. Pleasure boats dot the 5.6 – square – km lake every day. Gardens of a classic style on three lake islands are big attractions for tourists. Around the lake are numerous scenic spots and sites of historical interest.

Sanya, a city at the southern tip of Hainan Island in the South China Sea

Not too far from the West Lake is a new scenic area called Qiandao Lake, or Thousand – Island Lake. The lake, which is ten times larger than the West Lake, is dotted with 1,078 islands, big and small. Among them are Deer Island, Monkey Island and Snake Island. The area is also known as "Green Qiandao Lake" since the vast expanse of water is surrounded by green mountains. The lake holds great attraction for tourists.

A vast country, China offers great diversity in

scenery and sights. South of the Yangtze are regions of rivers and lakes with a perennial green beauty, whereas in northwest China are the rugged, dry Loess Plateau and the seemingly endless Gobi desert. When Heilongjiang province in northeast China is a world of snow and ice, beaches in Hainan Island in the south are crowded with swimmers.

On the Gobi of northwest China, a motorist would not see a single person over a long distance. Sometimes, a faintly visible town would appear at a distance and, upon being approached, would disappear mysteriously — that is nothing but a mirage. Coming to the Gobi, tourists living in noisy, cramped cities would be surprised at the vastness of the world.

In Heilongjiang in winter, people can go hunting in the forests and take part in many kinds of activities on snow or ice. There are several well – equipped ski slopes in the province. The province's annual snow and ice festival offers facilities for skating, ice hockey, sledding and driving ice boats. Tourists can also enjoy ice sculpture and figure skating.

At the same time, Sanya in Hainan Island is still a world of sunshine, sea water and beaches. Swimming, surfing, sailing and scuba diving are among activities of choice for pleasure seekers.

A bull-against-bull fight, a sport enjoyed by the Miaos

甘　　肃
Gansu

直升飞机场
Heliport

南坪
Nanping

九寨沟风景区
Jiuzhaigou's Scenic Area

陕　西
Shaanxi

黄龙风景区
Huanglong (Yellow Dragon) Scenic Area

牟尼沟风景区
Munigou Scenic Area

▲雪宝鼎　5588米
Xuebaoding(Snow-capped Top) 5588m

四　川
Sichuan

成
都
—
九
寨
沟
直
升
机
航
线
Chengdu-Jiuzhaigou Coptor Route

剑门关风景区
Jianmen Pass
Scenic Area

绵阳
Mianyang

四姑娘山风景区　6250米
Siguniang mountain Scenic Area

绵竹
Mianzhu

都江堰
Dujiangyan

卧龙自然保护区
Wolong Nature Reserve

青城山
Qingchengshan (Green City Mountain)

成都
Chengdu

WITNESSING LIFESTYLES AND FOLK CUSTOMS

Tourists from overseas are not only interested in the Great Wall, the clay army of soldiers and horses and the landscape of Guilin, but also curious about the Chinese people. How do the Chinese nurtured in a 7,000 – year civilization live under a socialist system? How are the Chinese different from themselves in values, customs and lifestyles? Foreign tourists hope to acquire an on – the – spot understanding, and some would like to experience some of the customs and lifestyles.

When a group of American photographers visited the Palace Museum (the Forbidden City), they used about 30 percent of their film taking shots of the halls and buildings and about 70 percent taking pictures of fellow Chinese visitors.

At night, on cruise ships passing the Three Gorges of the Yangtze, foreign tourists are usually not particularly interested in dancing or singing, karaoke fashion. Rather, they like to talk with interpreters, tour guides or members of the crew. They are interested in subjects such as: how are Chinese families structured? How do three or four generations of the same family treat one another? What is the relationship between the members financially? How do the Chinese spend their spare time? How do boys and girls court one another? What is the percentage of divorces?

Foreign tourists form different impressions of different parts of China usually as a result of the different impressions they get of the local Chinese. For example, they usually have a fairly high opinion of their tours in Shanghai though the city does not have much in the way of natural landscape and places of historical interest. They think that people in Shanghai are more open and warmer in attitude. Many locals can and like to speak English with foreigners. They are ready to give directions to any foreign traveler.

With a better understanding of what foreign tourists want, travel agencies in China have emphasized the inclusion of Chinese customs and lifestyles when developing tour products.

Wuxi, a city in southern Jiangsu, offers a tour program called "Cruise on the Ancient Canal."

Touring a Beijing hutong, or alley

Cruising on the north - south Grand Canal with a history of more than 1,000 years is an exciting experience. But, for tourists, more exciting is perhaps to see how people along the canal live. The canal in downtown Wuxi is a narrow waterway flanked by residential houses. Tourists on board a cruise ship can see, at very close range, old people feeding birds and watering flowers, old women sorting vegetables and washing clothes, and children doing homework or playing. Sometimes the old people and children would raise their head and greet the tourists.

In Beijing there is a tour program called "Roaming the Hutongs." Hutongs are back alleys where Chinese life can be seen at its most typical and traditional. Tourists take rides on tricycles that are pedaled along old, narrow hutongs. In winter, they will see groups of old men basking in the sun and chatting and little girls skipping rubber bands; and in summer, they will hear the sound of cicadas from trees that line hutongs and the hawking of watermelons. By arrangement by a travel agency, tourists can visit a family living in a courtyard house. Guests and host can have tea or make jiaozi (dumpling) together.

In Shanghai, there is a tour item called "Spending a Day as a Shanghai Citizen." That means the tourist actually lives in an old - fashioned row house or a new apartment in the city. Early in the morn-

ing, he or she, together with his or her host, will walk the host's child to school, buy the day's food, haggle with peddlers and, back at home, cook the food. He or she will certainly learn from the host how to make one or two Chinese dishes. In the afternoon, the guest will sip tea and chat with the host. In the evening, he or she will have supper together with all the members of the host family. Supper is followed by a period of total relaxation: while the TV is on, the guest and members of the host family will have a lively conversation, all the while cracking melon or sunflower seeds. Foreign tourists having had the experience say that the 24 hours they spent as "a Shanghai Citizen" were the height of their China tour and that they would never forget the experience.

Customs and lifestyles differ in different places

in China. At the request of tourists, travel agencies can organize visits to factories, villages, kindergartens, homes for the aged and farmers' markets.

If tourists happen to visit China in a period with traditional holidays, they will have extra fun. In China, the longest and most important holiday is the Spring Festival, or New Year's Day of the lunar calendar, which falls usually in late January or early February. Like Christmas in the West, the Spring Festival is a time for family reunion. On new year's eve, all members of a family gather around the dinner table and share a "New Year's Eve Meal," which usu-

ally consists of jiaozi, or dumplings, in the north and dishes and rice in the south. They also watch a special TV program, usually a variety show, being broadcast by the China Central Television Station. In many places, people send away the old year and welcome the new by setting off firecrackers. The first few days of the new year are for visits between relatives and friends. It is a time when children wear new clothes and new hats and expect cash gifts from grown – ups.

During the Spring Festival, celebrations with local characteristics are held everywhere in the

Shanghai sight: modernity comes side by side with tradition

country. Activities include drum dances, lion dances and walking on stilts. In Beijing, on the grounds of numerous temples are held fairs where people watch traditional performances, eat snacks and buy handicraft articles. Tourists, mingling with local people at such fairs, will experience the joyous atmosphere of the Chinese New Year.

After the lunar New Year is the Lantern Festival, which falls on the fifteenth day of the first month of the lunar year. On the day, people across China eat a round - shaped dumpling called yuanxiao in the north and tangyuan in the south. Made of glutinous rice with various kinds of stuffing, the dumpling is a symbol of harmony in the family and success in business. Lantern dances and parades are usual activities in many places on the day of the festival. Some lantern dances feature huge dragons wielded about by dozens of people simultaneously. Best - known lantern festivals are those in Quanzhou, Fujian province, and Zigong, Sichuan province.

The fifth day of the fifth lunar month (usually in June) is the Dragon Boat Festival. The traditional food on the day is called zongzi, a pyramid –shaped dumpling made of glutinous rice wrapped in bamboo or reed leaves. The most exciting activity on the day is of course the dragon boat race. Participating in each race are usually dozens of long, narrow dragon boats, each of

Watching a lion dance,
a traditional New Year
performance

A folk performance celebrating the Chinese New Year

which is rowed by dozens of people. Amid roars of encouragement from spectators on both banks, rowers exert their strength to the greatest extent, propelling their boats forward at a high speed. Some foreign tourists come to China specially to see dragon boat races.

On the fifteenth day of the eighth lunar month (usually in September) is the Mid – Autumn Festival. The Chinese believe that the moon is brighter and rounder on the day than on any others in the year, and they have the habit of gazing at the moon and eating the moon cake on the day. Travel agencies now offer "Enjoying the Moon on the Mid – Autumn Festival" program to tourists. In Hangzhou and Wuxi, tourists spend the evening of the day under a full moon on ships that float on the West Lake and the Taihu Lake. To the accompaniment of local music, they sample local

Making jiaozi, or meat-stuffed dumplings, a food popular in northern China

food and see how moonlight plays with the water.

Other holidays include the New Year's Day (January 1), the Women's Day (March 8), the Labor Day (May 1), the Children's Day (June 1), the Teachersí Day (September 10), the National Day (October 1) and the Double Ninth Festival (the 9th day of the 9th lunar month, a day for height climbing and paying respect to the aged).

China is a multi – ethnic country. Aside from the Han, the country has 55 minority nationalities. They live mainly in border provinces and regions in the northeastern, northwestern and southwestern parts of the country. These regions are all open to foreign tourists. As long as tourists are not afraid of hardships on the way, they can visit any village in these regions and experience the local lifestyle.

The Xishuangbanna area of Yunnan province, southwest China, has a concentration of ethnic Dais, who live in bamboo cottages erected along rivers and lakes. A Dai cottage, which usually has two stories supported by several wooden columns, has a thatched roof and is surrounded by bamboo and bajiao banana groves. There is peace and quietness all around.

Dai men like to tattoo their bodies. Typically, a Dai man wears a white coat buttoned at the front and a white head scarf. Dai women like to wear a bright - colored close - fitting jacket covered by a long - sleeved short coat and a sheath skirt. They tie their hair into a high bun and adorn their hair with flowers. They look especially attractive when, standing in a shallow river, they wash their long hair. The Dais believe in Hinayana

The dragon boat race is about to start. Dragon boat races are held on the 5th day of the 5th lunar month, or the Dragon Boat Festival, in many parts of the country.

Buddhism and Dai parents like to have their boys study Buddhist scriptures. At the age of seven or eight, boys are sent to monasteries as apprentice monks and resume secular life at the age of 20. Only people having spent time in a monastery as a monk have social status. Tourists will see Buddhist pagodas in every village and kasaya – clad monks, old and young, wherever they go.

The Dai people are good at dancing and singing. Dancers usually simulate animal movements. For tourists, a good way to enjoy themselves in a Dai area is to watch the Peacock Dance and the Elephant – Foot Drum Dance, while tasting rice cooked in bamboo tubes and steamed meat wrapped in bajiao banana leaves. Souvenirs with Dai characteristics include painted wooden boats, hand – woven brocade and bamboo – woven handicraft articles.

In Xishuangbanna, the tourist high tide is the Water – Sprinkling Festival that falls on April 13 – 15 of the Dai calendar – new year's holidays for the Dais. The Dai people regard water as the god of all life and the symbol of purity, goodness and brightness. That is why they sprinkle water at the beginning of a new year as a way of praying for happiness. Carrying pails and basins filled with water, the local people, old and young, male and female, joined by tourists, run after and throwing water at one another. The more water one gets, the more happi-

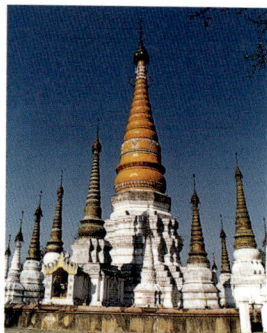

ness he or she is supposed to receive. All are soaked through at the end of a session. During the Water – Sprinkling Festival, the Dais also hold dragon boat races and song – and – dance evening parties as well as let off fireworks.

The Miaos live in the neighboring Guizhou province. They reside in "suspension" houses built on slopes. Viewed from the front, these have two stories with wooden supports, and viewed from behind, they have just one story of a wooden structure. The Miaos store their fire wood and keep animals on the lower floor and have their own room on the upper floor. Miao villages are surrounded by trees and terraced fields.

Miao men grow long hair and wrap a towel

round their head. They wear collar - less, big - sleeved coats and loose trousers. Miao women tie their hair into a bun and wrap their head with a towel. They wear pleated skirt, usually of green and blue colors. During holidays women wear silver ornaments on almost all parts of their body – hands, chest and back, for example. As they walk, the ornaments, which may weigh as much as several kilograms, shine with light and produce a jingling sound.

When tourists go to a Miao village as guests, the villagers will meet them outside the village. The men will stand on a slope playing a wind instrument called Lusheng as part of their welcoming ceremony. The women wearing their holiday best will sing and dance and offer the guests wine contained in ox horns. On their way to the village, more wine will be offered, as "Block - the-

Miao women in their holiday best

Way Wine," "Enter - the - Village Wine" and "Welcome Wine." The villagers will stage a formal performance for the guests. The guests then will be
invited by individual families to drink wine and
have a meal. Traditional food includes pickled
vegetables, fish with pickled vegetables and soup
with pickled vegetables. Wine is brewed at home,
from rice. Villagers will paint a "lucky mole" onto
the face of the guests and dance with them. For
the tourists, this is usually the climax of their day
with the Miaos.

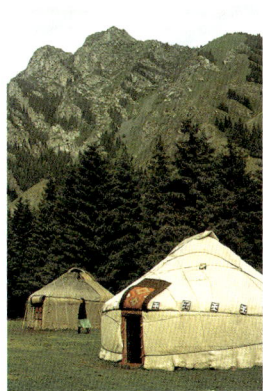

Kasak yurts at the foot
of the Tianshan range

Sometimes, Miao villagers will stage for their
guests a bull fight which is normally put up only
on special holidays. Here, a bull fight is a fight
between bulls, not one between a bull and a man,
as in Spain.

Miao women's handicraft includes batik, embroidery and cross - stitch work - materials for
clothes and ornamental articles. Tourists love to
see Miao women do their handicraft and some of
them would like to have a try. Some handicraft
articles are souvenirs very much treasured by
tourists.

Mongolians living in the vast grasslands of northern China have different customs and a different
lifestyle. Most Mongolians live in yurts. The yurt,
round - shaped and movable, is a wood - wicker
structure covered with a thick felt. It is a bulwark
against sun shine, rain, storms, ice and snow.

All Mongolians, male and female, old and young, wear long – sleeved and high – collared robes. Silks and satins of different colors are the usual fabric for such robes. Men prefer blue or brown robes, whereas women like such bright colors as red, green and purple. Both men and women wear waistbands outside their robes as well as leather boots. Men wear leather hats, while women wrap their head with colored silk scarves. On special occasions, women wear beautiful head ornaments, some of which are decorated with pearls, gold and silver pieces and precious stones.

For tourists going to the grassland of the Inner Mongolia Autonomous Region, a tour item is to live in a yurt equipped with modern sanitary facilities, drink milk tea and eat beef and mutton which they themselves cut from roasted carcasses, using Mongolian knives. The most popular guests will be those who like to drink liquor. For the hostess, it is a great pleasure to keep filling their cups.

Tourists can also watch Mongolian – style dancing, wrestling, horse racing and camel races. It is a pleasure, too, to hear Mongolians play ma tou qin, a bowed stringed instrument with a scroll carved like a horse's head. Of course, tourist can ride horses, shoot arrows, practice marksmanship and drive a Mongolian – style ox – cart called le le

The Torch Festival of the Yi ethnic people.

che. At night, lying on the grass and seeing a sky
studded with stars, a city dweller would feel being one with heaven and earth.

Most Uygurs live in the central Asian region
of Xinjiang. Kashgar, a border city in the region,
has a concentration of Uygurs. Rich with ethnic
Uygur flavors, the city has been quite attractive to
tourists.

The typical wear for Uygur men is a buttonless
robe outside a shirt with the robe tied at the waist
with a long girdle; that for women is a bright - colored dress covered by a jacket. All Uygurs, men and
female, old and young, like to wear small four -
pointed embroidered caps as well as boots. Women
like to put on makeup, and wear jewelry and bright
- colored scarves. A Uygur girl usually has eight or
a dozen pig - tails. The longer the pig - tails, the
more beautiful its owners are regarded.

The Uygurs live in one - storied flat - roofed

houses made of clay. The roof is used for drying crops and for family members to enjoy cool air in summer. Inside the house are tapestries covering the walls and built – in wardrobes. Inside and around the courtyard grow plants, flowers and fruit trees. The Uygurs are a hospitable people. Tourists, as guests, are treated to melons, fruit and many kinds of traditional food. The most typical may be the Whole Sheep Barbecue and zhua fan – cooked rice mixed with meat and eaten with hands.

Early morning on every Sunday sees people in Kashgar flocking to the bazaar to see or buy handicraft articles, melons, vegetables, fruit and livestock, big and small. People haggle over prices for Uygur caps, knives and silk fabrics.

The most mysterious ethnic minority group is perhaps the Mosuos whose lifestyle still has vestiges of a matriarchal society. They live by Lake Lugu at a Sichuan – Yunnan border area, which is now open

A Mosuo a'zhu, or loving couple, having a boat ride on Lake Lugu. The Mosuos live in a Sichuan-Yunnan border area, southwest China.

to foreign tourists.

The Mosuos follow a form of marriage called a'zhu. Men and women choose the object of their love freely, and the relationship can be short and long. A man and woman having established an a'zhu relationship continue to live separately, in their respective mothers' homes. The only difference is that the man spends the night with his woman in the latter's home and leaves at dawn. All their offspring are raised by the woman's side. Every Mosuo family is headed by a woman, who is in charge of production and wealth distribution. Men living in their mother's home are in a subordinate position. Historians and sociologists regard this practice as "a living fossil of the primitive marriage form."

Mosuo houses are made of logs placed one on the other. The upper floor, partitioned into several bedrooms, is used as human dwelling, whereas the ground floor is for keeping livestock. On the upper floor is also an Islamic scripture hall since the Mosuos believe in Islam.

In March, April and July, the Mosuos hold mountain – and sea – worshipping ceremonies by Lake Lugu. Crowds of people, while going round the lake, chant scriptures and pay respect to the Lion Mountain nearby. At night, people cook food on bonfires and sleep outdoors. It is a time of courtship for young men and women.

EXPERIENCING RICH CHINESE CULTURE

China with a history of 7,000 years has a rich culture. In ancient times, despite unbelievable difficulties and hardships involved in international travels, many people, intentionally or unintentionally, engaged in cultural exchanges across national boundaries. They included businessmen, priests, monks, scholars and even officers and soldiers fighting wars. China, while absorbing the cultures of other nations, has naturally spread its rich and unique culture outside its boundaries.

Twenty – two centuries ago, Zhang Qian of the Han Dynasty opened the Silk Road that linked China with central Asia and Europe. Apart from silk that had been introduced to the West by way of the Silk Road, other Chinese products and skills that spread successively westward along the Road include sericulture, gunpowder, the compass, copper smelting, papermaking, typographic printing, tea, peach, pear, citrus fruit and barley.

Twelve centuries ago, Monk Jianzhen of the Tang Dynasty went to Japan, taking with him 85 craftsmen good at carving jade, painting pictures, carving Buddhist figures, engraving, embroidering, engraving tablets and other lines of creative work. When he was in Japan, aside from helping local religious circles standardize Buddhist disciplines, the Chinese monk spread knowledge about Chinese architecture, the art of carving and medical practices, among other things. As a matter of fact, China began having contacts with Japan and Korea as early as in the Qin Dynasty 2,000 years ago. Advanced Chinese skills such as sericulture, silk reeling and pottery making had spread eastward long before Monk Jianzhen's Japan travel.

Five hundred years ago, in the Ming Dynasty, Zheng He in command of a giant Chinese fleet made seven voyages westward across the South China Sea and the Indian Ocean within a span of

The Monk Jianzhen Memorial Hall in Yangzhou's Daming (Great Brightness) Monastery is testimony to Chinese-foreign cultural exchanges in history. The Tang Dynasty monk taught Buddhism in Japan in the 8th century.

28 years. The fleet covered more than 50,000 km in total and reached more than 30 countries and regions in Asia and Africa. This is a big event in the world navigation history. Zheng's voyages also facilitated cultural exchanges.

Today, tourists can find traces of Chinese – foreign cultural exchanges at countless sites – along the old Silk Road from Shaanxi and Gansu to Xinjiang, at the Daming Temple in Yangzhou where Monk Jianzhen once served as abbot, and Zheng He the Navigator's residence and tomb in Nanjing.

Official and non – official cultural exchanges over thousands of years have led to a gradual emergence of a "Han cultural sphere" in China and its neighboring countries and regions. The influence of this culture has spread to the rest of the world in varying degrees.

That is why almost all tourists from outside China have heard or read about stories and legends about the Orient and, invariably, can find their verification in one way or another during their China tour.

Striking the ancient bell in Suzhou's Hanshan (Cool Hill) Temple to usher in a new year.

Chinese – language newspapers in many countries often carry Confucius' teachings such as "There must be a teacher for me out of every three – person group," "Reviewing the past helps one understand the present," "Judging a person by not only listening to what he says but also

watching what he does," and "Do not do unto people what you would not have others do unto you." A statue of Confucius stands in New York's China Town. "Confucius" has become a word in many languages and is included in dictionaries of many a language.

Confucius, who lived 2,500 years ago, was a great thinker and educator. As founder of Confucianism, he was one of a few people who have exerted the greatest influence in the cultural history of the world. His teachings have continued to influence the Chinese people and people of Chinese origin elsewhere in the world in their thinking and behavior. Academic circles in the

Confucius Temple, a symbol of respect commanded by Confucianism throughout the ages in China. The temple, together with the residence and cemetery of the Confucius family, is listed as a World Cultural Heritage site by the UN Educational, Scientific and Cultural Organization.

West have never stopped their research on Confucianism. Lun Yu, or "Confucian Analects," which records the teachings of Confucius, has been regarded as a Confucian classic.

Qu Fu in Shandong province is Confucius' hometown. Tourist attractions there are the Confucius Residence, the Confucius Temple and the Confucian Family Cemetery. China International Travel Service often organize Confucian culture training classes for foreign tour groups in Qu Fu. Trainees are taught the six attainments advocated by Confucius: adherence to social and ethical norms, music playing, arrow shooting, taking the reins of horses pulling carriages, reading and doing arithmetic. On the 26th day of the ninth lunar month every year, the birthday of Confucius, a cultural festival in memory of the great thinker is held in Qu Fu.

Midnight on December 31 every year will find

Learning shadow boxing on board a pleasure ship

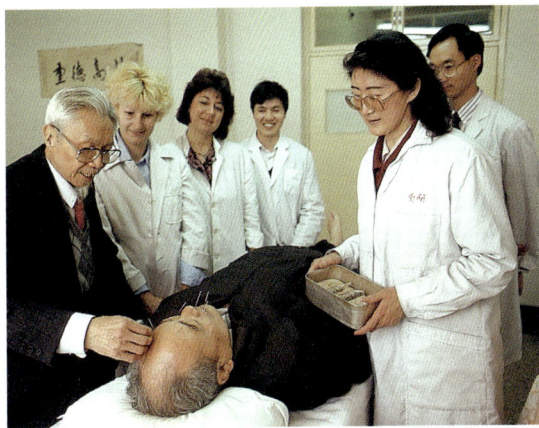

Traditional Chinese medicine appeals to doctors among foreign tourists.

hundreds of Japanese tourists gathered at the Hanshan (Cool Hill) Temple in Suzhou. They are there to hear the 108 peals of the bell that usher in the new year. This annual gathering at the Hanshan Temple has been a regular tour program for the last decade and more. In a textbook for senior middle school students in Japan is a poem written by a Tang Dynasty (618 – 907) Chinese poet named Zhang Ji. The poem, entitled "Berthed by the Maple – Shaded Bridge for the Night," reads: "The crows caw when the moon goes down; nothing is discernible except a shimmering layer of frost. Looking at maple trees lining the river and lights coming from fishing boats, the traveler, overcome by sadness, cannot go to sleep. Nearby is the Hanshan Temple outside the city of Suzhou; peals of the temple bell reach the passenger boat at midnight." Almost all Japanese who have received at least a senior middle school

Monks of Henan's Shaolin Temple practicing Shaolin kungfu. Shaolin kungfu dates back to the Tang Dynasty.

education are familiar with the poem and many would like to visit the temple and its surroundings.

In fierce market competition, commercial businesses in Japan are often said to use various political and military strategies as described by the Chinese classic novel "Romance of the Three Kingdoms" and military strategies and tactics summarized by Sun Tse, an ancient Chinese military strategist, in a book entitled "Sun Tse's Military Strategies." Along the "Three Kingdoms Tour Route" traversing Jiangsu, Hubei, Sichuan and Henan can often been seen Japanese tourists who, with "Romance of the Three Kingdoms" in hand, are looking for sites described in the book. The route has also attracted tourists from other countries and regions in the "Han cultural sphere" and from the West.

Wushu, or kungfu, also holds appeal to foreign tourists. The Shaolin Temple and Chenjiagou Village in Dengfeng County, Henan, have been destinations for foreign tourists wishing to learn Shaolin boxing or explore the origin of the boxing. There, they can not only witness shows of genuine kungfu but also become trainees in a wushu school or wushu club.

Taiji in wushu (taiji is a mysterious term which may mean, among other things, the essence of life), qigong (deep – breathing exercises) and acupuncture are traditional Chinese ways of keeping fit and curing diseases. Many foreign tourists have heard of them and come to China to learn the skills or have one ailment or another treated in traditional Chinese ways.

In some countries in the East, people use pointed brushes dipped in black ink for writing and painting. This has its origin in China. In Chinese calligraphy, there are almost half a dozen forms of handwriting called zhuan, di, kai, hang and cao (cursive). The Chinese art of painting has categories of ink and wash, paintings on silk and new year pictures. In style of creation, some artists use freehand brushwork characterized by vivid expression and bold outline, while others pay meticulous attention to details. Subjects of paintings include human beings,

The Monkey King, a shadow play character

landscape, plants and flowers, fruit, birds, animals, fish and insects.

The writing brush, the ink slab, paper and ink used for writing and painting are called "Four Treasures of the Study." Writing brushes produced in Huzhou are the best. They are made of choice goat hair, rabbit hair or weasel hair. The best ink slabs come from Zhaoqing, Guangdong. Xuan paper and Hui ink sticks are produced in Anhui, and unique skills and processes are used in their production, which has had a long history. Foreign tourists interested in China's traditional stationery like to visit places where the best "treasures of the study" are produced. There, they can witness their production with traditional skills and buy their own "four treasures of the study."

Making personal seals is a unique Chinese cultural phenomenon. When in China, some foreign tourists would ask their interpreters to translate their names into Chinese characters and have them engraved on seals made usually of choice Qingtian stone or Shoushan stone. A seal of this kind is a good souvenir.

The earliest china was made in China. In English, except for a difference in the case of the first letter, china meaning porcelain utensils and China meaning the country are one and the same word. The rest of the world regards China as the porcelain country. Naturally, Jingdezhen city —

Da Ah Fu, or the Lady of Happiness–a folk handicraft article made in Hangzhou that symbolizes happiness

the capital of porcelain in China — has a strong appeal for foreign tourists.

In Jingdezhen, tourists will find sites of kilns for the firing of porcelain that existed hundreds of years ago as well as highly - valued ancient porcelain and porcelain pieces that have been unearthed from such sites. A tourist can also, under the direction of a local craftsman, make a bowl himself, carve his name on it and have it fired in a kiln for hours. That will make an excellent souvenir to take home.

Since Julius Caesar in ancient Rome donned his toga made of silk 2,000 years ago, people in the West have known that, in the faraway East, there is a country called China which can produce such beautiful fabric. Suzhou and Hangzhou,

Fujian's round buildings-ancient residences which used to house a single big family each

Buying porcelain in China, the land of chinaware

well – known silk producers in China, are where international travelers go to explore the mysteries of silk.

For a group of tourists, an itinerary in Suzhou or Hangzhou may include a silk museum, a village where people raise silkworms, a silk factory and a workshop where people do embroidery on silk fabric. Naturally, when they want to buy silk products, tourists have a wide range of choices.

Various forms of folk art and handicraft articles have special attractions for some foreign tourists. They include papercuts, puppet shows (with puppets made of donkey hide), lanterns, kites and fans.

Today, not only is there traditional Chinese architecture in Japan, the Republic of Korea and countries in Southeast Asia, but people can find Chinese – style arches, pavilions and gardens in the United States, Canada, France and Australia.

Choosing silk products in Hangzhou

"Ming Xuan" in the Metropolitan Museum of Art in New York is a replica of a courtyard in a traditional Suzhou garden, the Wang Shi Yuan.

Chinese restaurants are now found everywhere in the world. Many people in the West are quite adept at using chopsticks. They seem to have a special liking for Chinese food and eat a big feast in a Chinese restaurant with family members or friends once in a while. Owing to historical reasons, Cantonese cuisine dominates in Chinese restaurants in foreign countries.

Chinese – style catering is part of Chinese culture and has a long history. There are four major cuisines in the country: Shandong, Sichuan, Cantonese and Huaiyang (Jiangsu), which together have more than 5,000 dishes on their formal menus. The four cooking styles have numerous branches. In addition, provinces and ethnic minority regions have their own unique cooking styles. People patronizing Chinese restaurants in foreign countries cannot possibly have an overall knowledge of Chinese cuisine. And, besides, thanks to the influence of local dietary habits, what they eat in such restaurants may not have been prepared according to a truly authentic Chinese cooking style. It is only in China that people can sample authentic Chinese food and experience its great diversity.

The Chinese regard eating and drinking a culture, namely food culture. Attention is paid not only to the color, fragrance and taste of food and drinks but also to the environment and atmo-

Dishes prepared according to royal recipes at the Fangshan (Imitation Imperial Kitchen) Restaurant in Beihai Park, Beijing

sphere in which food and drinks are consumed. To enjoy the best of China's food culture, one has to eat an authentic Chinese dinner served in a Chinese garden house.

Snacks in Beijing

It is often said that, for a foreigner, a Beijing tour is not complete if he or she fails to do three things: climb to the Great Wall, taste the Beijing roast duck and see a Peking Opera performance.

Peking Opera is a unique Chinese theatrical art that combines singing and dancing, including acrobatics. The most intriguing thing about Peking Opera is its abstract way of conveying meanings: the stage is bare, but an actor or actress, with movements and expressions accompanied by music, makes the audience feel that he or she is opening a door, riding a horse or being carried in a sedan chair, and enables them to follow the development of the plot. It is quite often that several actors on a bare stage can create the scene of a huge army going to war.

In Peking Opera performances staged especially for foreign tourists, usually action plays are selected so that the language barrier does not pose too much of a problem. These include "San Cha Kou" (the Crossroads), "Shi Yu Zhuo" (Story of the Jade Bracelets), "Da Nao Tian Gong" (Wrecking Havoc in the Heavens) and "Gui Fei Zui Jiu" (The Concubine Gets Drunk). Colorful costume, a great array of masks for different kinds of characters and traditional Chinese musical accompaniment make foreign audiences intrigued and entertained.

Provinces and regions in the country have their own local operas, such as Wu Opera in Shanghai, Yue Opera in Zhejiang, Huangmei Opera in Anhui, Lu Opera in Shandong, Ji Opera in Jilin, Ping Opera in Hebei, Yu Opera in Henan, Yue Opera in Guangdong and Chuan Opera in Sichuan. Other performances with a strong local flavor are Imitation Tang Dance in Xi'an, Shaanxi province, and Story of the Silk Road (a dance) in Lanzhou, Gansu province.

Chinese acrobatic troupes have won a great number of prizes at annual international acrobatics festivals. Acrobatics has a history of more than 2,000 years in China. Rich with an oriental flavor are foot – and – leg skill, head – support skill and

An acrobatic performance

saucer playing. Big cities such as Beijing, Shanghai, Wuhan and Guangzhou all have their own acrobatic troupes.

Since its introduction into China from India,
Buddhism has gradually branched out into different sects with Chinese characteristics including
Tiantan, Huayan, Chan (Zen) and Pure Land. And,
from China, Buddhism spread to Japan via Korea.
For Japanese and Korean Buddhists, therefore,
the origin of their religion is in China. Every year,
Japanese and Korean Buddhist groups come to
China to worship Buddhist shrines where their
sects had their origin. In recent years, some ac-
complished Chinese Buddhist monks have gone
to countries in Europe and North America at the
invitation of local believers of Chinese descent to
take charge of religious affairs at local monaster-

Peking Opera, which
has a history of more
than 200 years.

ies. This has quickened the spread of Buddhism in those countries.

There are in China four mountains that are sacred to Buddhist believers: the Wutai in Shanxi, the E'mei in Sichuan, the Jiuhua in Anhui and the Putuo in Zhejiang. These mountains are dotted with monasteries and temples filled daily with worshippers; and they all have unrivaled natural beauty. Many groups of foreign Buddhists go there to worship every year. Large numbers of ordinary tourists visit the mountains, too, thanks to their rich Buddhist culture and natural beauty.

The religion that was born in China and is unique to the country is Taoism, which has had a history of more than 1,800 years. The essence of Taoism is respect for nature. Among Taoist concepts are : "Human beings follow the earth, the earth follows the heaven, the heaven follows the way of the world, and the way of the world follows nature." The power of nature, Taoists believe, invigorates human beings. The Taoist back – to – nature belief coincides with that of today's tourists.

Mountains regarded as sacred by Taoists include Laoshan in Shandong, Maoshan in Jiangsu, Qingchengshan in Sichuan, and Wudangshan in Hubei. Well – known Taoist temples are Baiyun in Beijing, Xuanmiao in Suzhou, Zhongyue in Henan and Mazu in Fujian's Meizhou. They attract tourists interested in Taoist culture.

Tibetan lamas at a
religious ceremony

REFORM AND OPEN POLICIES BOOST THE DEVELOPMENT OF TOURISM

Tourism dates back to ancient times. In China, it can be traced to the Spring and Autumn and Warring States periods 2,500 years ago. Tourism in a modern sense, however, did not begin until 1841, when Thomas Cook, a Briton, organized a group of people for travels in accordance with a schedule and itinerary and at a packaged price, using the just – invented train as the means of transportation. Tourism has since developed gradually.

During the first half of the 20th century, tourism remained largely stagnated owing to the two world wars. After the Second World War, tourism quickly recovered and gradually became a routine social activity. Tourism, which was at first attached to other trades, became an independent industry.

After the 1950s, with rapid economic development in some countries, people's income and paid holidays kept increasing. Jet passenger aircraft that first appeared in 1959 have made international and inter – continental travels easier and faster. These factors have stimulated the development of international tourism. Since the beginning of the 1990s, as people's ideas about consumption have changed, their income increased and transportation improved, tourism has become a popular activity from a luxury formerly enjoyed by a privileged few only. And tourism has entered a stage of development. According to statistics released by WTO in March 1998, the year of 1997 saw a total of 617 million people worldwide taking international tours, and revenues of the world tourist industry during the year, not including air fares, reached US$435 billion.

China's tourist industry has had ups and downs over the past several decades.

The industry in its modern sense started in Shanghai in the early 20th century. In 1923, a savings bank in Shanghai established a tour division, which later separated itself from the bank to become

Foreign tourists choose handicraft articles inside a Dai-style bamboo cottage.

The Mausoleum of Genghis Khan in Ejin Horo Banner, Inner Mongolia

China Travel Agency thanks to growing business. The travel agency later established branches in more than 20 cities in the country and offices in some Southeast Asian countries. But China at that time lacked conditions to develop a tourist industry owing to its backward economy and incessant civil wars.

After the founding of New China in 1949, an increasing number of overseas Chinese and Chinese compatriots in Hong Kong and Macao visited the country. Also on the increase were foreigners visiting China by invitation. Under the circumstances, China International Travel Service (CITS) was founded in 1954.

CITS, China's first national travel agency, began signing business cooperation agreements with its counterparts in the Soviet Union and some East European countries; it also established business ties with travel agencies in France and other Western countries with a view to receiving travelers paying their own way. During the three years from 1956 through 1958, CITS received more than 10,000 self – paying foreign travelers. The number of CITS branches had by then increased from the original 12 to 35, which are located in all major domestic cities. A national network serving foreign tourists had by then taken shape.

In the early 1960s, China's domestic political and economic situation took a turn for the better and, internationally, new changes had taken place. In 1964, Chinese Premier Zhou Enlai visited 14 African countries; China established diplomatic relations with France; and direct air traffic was established between China and Pakistan. With the air route serving as a bridge between China and the rest of the world, the number of people traveling to China increased. In 1965, CITS received 12,877 foreign tourists, a historical record.

Site of the Kingdom of Tsada Guge in Tibet's Ngari. The castle of 11 storeys was built in the 10th century.

At that time, tourism in China was regarded as a form of "people's diplomacy," that is to say, tourism was intended to attract foreigners to visit China, thereby promoting understanding and friendship between the Chinese people and people of other countries. The year of 1965 saw the establishment of China State Administration for Travel and Tourist Affairs, the predecessor of China National Tourism Administration (CNTA).

The Cultural Revolution that started in 1966 brought China's nascent tourism to a halt. It is not until 1971 when China resumed exchanges in the field of tourism with Romania, Yugoslavia and other East European countries that China's tourist industry took a turn for the better. During the year, 30 self - paying Americans visited New China, ending a situation where mutual tourist visits between China and the United Sates had been zero.

The true rise of a tourist industry in China began in the late 1970s, when economic development took center stage, reform unfolded in every sector and the country opened its door to the rest of the world. People, especially those in the West, were eager to see what the long - closed China looked like, and they came to the country in ever increasing numbers. This has given rise to an international tourist industry in the country.

In terms of tourist resources, China is among the world's richest. Its rich natural, cultural and

Shanghai: the
Bund at night

social resources have great appeal to tourists. And the Chinese are a hospitable people. The policies of reform and opening have enabled China to gradually tap its potential in tourism.

The Chinese government has decided to develop the country's tourist industry "appropriately in advance." That is to say, it should develop at a pace slightly faster than that for the national economy as a whole; and, by the year 2000, while other Chinese industries are expected to reach technological levels reached by developed countries in the early 1980s, it should be on a par with its advanced international counterparts in terms of management, technology and the quality of services. By then, China hopes to become a devel-

The Chinese Cultural Village, a park in Shenzhen featuring villages of China's ethnic minority groups. Picture shows the Dong village in the park.

oped country in tourism.

To achieve this goal, the Chinese government has called for developing tourism by all quarters and sectors (the state, localities, government departments, collectives and individuals), by self – reliance and by utilizing foreign funds. Tourist enterprises enjoy tax reduction or exemption in the period of their initial operation, according to government policies.

At the same time, the Chinese government has made it clear that the country's tourist industry should be one with Chinese characteristics. By "Chinese characteristics" are meant the following:

First, tourism in China is not only an industry but also a "window" for an open China and a bridge for the promotion of friendship. Tourism can enable the rest of the world to have a better understanding of China and enhance friendship between the Chinese people and peoples of other countries. At the same time, tourism is expected to strengthen ties between the Chinese people and their compatriots in Hong Kong, Macao and Taiwan and Overseas Chinese.

Second, to offer diversified tour programs by taking advantage of the country's rich tourist resources. Such resources include the country's brilliant culture, beautiful natural scenery and great variety of folk customs and lifestyles. Programs include cruise on the Three Gorges section of the Yangtze, cruise on the Yellow River, cruise on the Grand Canal, the Silk Road tour, keep – fit tours where participants learn traditional Chinese skills such as shadow boxing,

A vacation village in Qingdao

acupuncture, massage and qigong (deep - breathing exercises), tours where participants learn Chinese cooking, exchange Chinese calligraphic skills, spend days with a Chinese family or fly kites, tours involving mountain climbing in Tibet, and tours on Inner Mongolia pastureland.

Third, tourist hotels and other tourist facilities should have a strong Chinese style as well as local flavors. For example, where conditions permit, the country's tourist industry has built courtyard - style hotels, hotels with a traditional garden setting found in Jiangsu and Zhejiang, yurt - style hotels, hotels shaped like the two - storied bamboo house of the Dai ethnic group, and hotels resembling cave houses found in northwest China. At the same time, the industry works hard to develop tourist souvenirs that have strong Chinese characteristics such as silk and embroidered pieces, woven and carved articles, cloisonne, ceramics and traditional Chinese paintings.

Fourth, services should reflect the ethics of China as a socialist country. The industry recommends healthy activities and bans gambling and prostitution. Tour providers will offer entertainment and sports activities with Chinese characteristics such as song - and - dance and opera performances, quyi (Chinese variety show), movies, acrobatics and wushu. At the same time, the industry will carry on the Chinese nation's tradition of hospitality and of-

The World Park in Beijing featuring miniature replicas of many famous sights in the world

fer the best of services to tourists.

With the promotion of the government and with the initiative of localities brought into full play, China's tourist industry has developed rapidly.

The mid – 1980s saw the development of tourist resources at a fairly big scale and on a selective basis. Major projects invested by the state include: expansion of the Museum of Qin Emperor Terra – Cotta Soldiers and Horses in Xi'an, water supplement for the Lijiang River in Guilin, renovation of the Qinhuai River Entertainment Center in Nanjing, expansion of Hanshan (Cool Hill) Temple in Suzhou, renovation of an ancient street at Zhenjiang's Xijingdu Ferry, dredging of Wuxi's ancient canal, construction of tourist facilities around Taihu Lake, construction in Hangzhou of a silk museum, a tea museum and a museum of traditional Chinese medicine, construction of a holiday complex at Yalong Beach in Hainan Island, repair of the Mutianyu section of the Great Wall in Beijing and the Jinshanling section of the Great Wall in Hebei, and renovation of the Yu Garden in the old town of Shanghai.

Major renovation and development projects invested and launched jointly by the state and local governments include: the Shanhaiguan Pass and the Jiayuguan Pass—the east and west extremes of the Great Wall, scenic areas along the Three Gorges section of the Yangtze river and along the Silk Road, a martial arts practicing hall at Shaolin Temple, a Song Dynasty Street in Kaifeng, a Water City at Penglai, Gengis Khan Mausoleum, Jiuzhaigou (Nine – Stockade Gully), Zhangjiajie Scenic Area in Hunan, and Huangguoshu Waterfalls in Guizhou.

At the same time, local governments developed many tourist facilities and areas with their own

A garden-styled hotel in Suzhou – the Zhuhui with a four-star rating

A courtyard-styled hotel in Beijing

money.

Since the beginning of the 1990s, a number of man – made sights have been constructed across the country. In Shenzhen bordering Hong Kong, for example, there are a park called "Beautiful China" that hosts all major architectural wonders in China in miniature form, a park called "Chinese Cultural Village" where young men and women from ethnic minority groups sing and dance for tourists, and a park called "Window on the World" that displays scenes from the five continents of the world. By the end of 1997, man – made theme parks had reached hundreds in number across the country.

In the early 1980s, there were only three travel

agencies in China: China International Travel Service, China Travel Service and China Youth Travel Service. With a dramatic increase in international tourist arrivals, the number of travel agencies shot up from three to 4,252 in 16 years. Many big travel agencies have each established dozens or even 100 – 200 branches across the country. These constitute a national tourist service network, one that is multi – functional and multi – tiered.

The years also saw an increase in the number of travel agencies catering to special – interest tourists. China Sports Tour Co., for example, has successfully organized mountain – climbing tours, and motorcycle and car rallies. Social circles having established special – interest travel agencies include workers' organizations, women's federations, and educational, cultural, commercial, shipping, gardening and handicraft sectors.

Travel agencies doing international business employ tour guides who speak foreign languages. Language services cover not only more common foreign tongues such as English, Japanese, French, German, Russian and Spanish but also less commonly – used ones including Korean, Malay, Thai, Arabic, Persian, Romanian, Portuguese and Swedish.

Most travel agencies are equipped with computers with which to optimize business volume, settle accounts, book reservations at hotels and

The "Buckingham Palace" inside Tianjin's New World Astor Hotel

on flights, do data processing and handle managerial affairs. A number of big travel agencies including China International Travel Service have entered the Internet, where they have hooked up with their counterparts overseas.

With regard to tourist hotels, China used to be extremely weak. Before 1949, the year when New China was founded, the country had only 19 hotels with 3,452 rooms in all that were up to international standard. The years after 1949 saw an increase in China's external exchanges. Apart from foreign government delegations, those visiting China included businessmen, professors, scholars, specialists, self – paying tourists and experts helping China with its economic development. To meet the demand for accommodation,

The five-star China World
Hotel in Beijing

provincial and municipal governments built a
number of hotels and guesthouses catering ex-
clusively to foreigners. By the end of 1978, the
number of such hotels across the country had
reached 137 with 15,500 rooms in all.

The years after 1979 saw an upsurge in international tourist business. Accommodation fell far short
of demand. As a result, construction of new hotels
accelerated — at a double – digit growth rate annually. At the same time, a star – rating system was
used to evaluate hotel quality. By the end of 1996,
the number of hotels that receive foreign tourists
had increased to 4,418 nationwide with a total of
594,000 rooms. Of these, 2,349 were rated as of a
star status, including 46 five – star hotels, 128 four
– star hotels, 743 three – star hotels, 1,148 two –
star hotels and 284 one – star hotels. Hotels in most
cities can now meet accommodation demand from

foreign tourists.

The first Sino – foreign joint venture established in an opening China is a tourist hotel — Jianguo Hotel in Beijing. This was followed by the establishment of more joint venture hotels in Shanghai, Tianjin and provincial cities. By the end of 1996, there were 694 Sino – foreign joint venture hotels and wholly – owned foreign hotels across the country, 15.7 percent of the total that receive foreign tourists. Thanks to a customer abundance, most joint – venture and wholly – owned foreign hotels have achieved good economic returns.

In the meantime, China has imported hotel equipment and introduced foreign hotel management expertise and services. International hotel chains such as Hilton, Sheraton and Holiday Inn have entered the Chinese market by establishing joint venture chain hotels in the country. Operating under a star – rating system based on international norms, all Chinese hotels try hard to meet international quality standards in terms of both equipment and services. Most three – star and better hotels, in particular, have reached international standards. Some five – star hotels have ranked among the world's best. These hotels include: Palace, China World, Great Wall, Chang Fu Gong Otani and Grand in Beijing, New Jingjiang, Portman, Garden, Huating and Jingan Hilton in Shanghai, White Swan, Dongfang, Great

Students of the Beijing Tourist Institute

China and Garden in Guangzhou, and Jingling in Nanjing.

The White Swan and Dongfang hotels in Guangzhou and Jingling Hotel in Nanjing are managed by Chinese themselves. Chinese managers, while applying foreign management expertise, have developed a Chinese – style hotel management system. Services in these hotels have a strong human touch, to the satisfaction of customers. As early as 1985, the White Swan Hotel was accepted by the "World's First – Rate Hotels" organization as a formal member. In 1986, Dongfang Hotel won a top prize from an international evaluation committee, of which "World's First – Class Hotels and Tourism" magazine of Spain was a member. Later, many other Chinese hotels won prizes at international competitions.

For the tourist industry, as for other industries, workforce competence is crucial.

Before the late 1970s, no institutions of higher

A foreign manager does her job at the Jianguo Hotel in Beijing.

Aspiring tour guides taking a qualifying examination

learning and secondary vocational schools in China had tourism as a speciality. In the early years of the tourist industry's development, most managerial and service personnel in the industry came from other lines of business.

The 1980s saw the establishment of tourism colleges and tourism vocational schools. They were jointly funded by the state and local governments. At present, there are 845 colleges and schools nationwide providing education on tourism. Among them, 166 are tourism colleges and institutions of higher learning teaching tourism as a speciality, 42 are tourism vocational schools, and 637 are middle schools providing tourism – related education. Total enrollment is 204,000. Beginning from the mid – 1980s, some institutions of higher learning began offering graduate studies on tourism.

Tourism schools have invited foreign tourism experts and professors to serve as teachers and, at the same time, send their own teachers abroad for training or further studies. In the meantime, dozens of textbooks have been compiled and published. In their compilation, foreign tourism textbooks have been used as reference and Chinese realities taken into account.

Aside from enrolling large numbers of senior and junior middle school graduates, tourism colleges and vocational schools provide training for tourism administrators as well as staff members and employees of tourist enterprises. A growing number of tour providers have begun applying a system whereby no employee is permitted to work unless he or she passes tests during training.

In 1983, China became a formal member of the World Tourism Organization (WTO).

Since 1978, the Chinese government has successively signed agreements on cooperation in the field of tourism with the governments of 23 countries. They include: Romania, Mexico, Malta, Egypt, Singapore, Cyprus, Hungary, Greece, Pakistan, the Philippines, Turkey, Kirgizstan, Cuba, Moldova, Tajikstan, Georgia, Thailand, Russia, Azarbayjan, Albania, Israel, Spain and Mongolia. The Chinese government has also signed bilateral memoranda of understanding on tourist cooperation with the governments of the United States, Sweden, Finland, Australia and Indonesia.

According to 1996 statistics, China National

Tourism Administration has set up offices in New York, Los Angeles, London, Paris, Frankfurt, Madrid, Sydney, Tokyo, Osaka and Singapore and a tour company in Hong Kong, offering consulting services for tourists. In 1997, the administration also set up offices in Toronto and Kathmandu. A total of 52 foreign travel agencies and tour companies have established 70 offices in Beijing, Shanghai, Guangzhou and Xiamen. They are based in Japan, the United Sates, Canada, Britain, Germany, Sweden, Norway, Thailand, the Republic of Korea, Singapore, Australia, Indonesia, the Philippines and Hong Kong. Some big Chinese travel agencies have also set up offices abroad.

Peking Opera masks

China's reform and open policies have made the country's tourist industry what it is today. In 1997, the industry reported total revenues of 311.22 billion yuan (US$37.5 billion), up 25.14 percent over the previous year. Tourist arrivals (including those from Hong Kong and Macao) increased from 5.7 million in 1980 to 57.59 million in 1997 (including those who did not stay at least one night in the country; those who did numbered 23.77 million); revenues in foreign exchange from the industry went up from US$617 million in 1980 to US$12.074 billion in 1997. Today, China ranks eighth in the world in tourism – sourced earnings and sixth in tourist arrivals.

CHINA IS NO LONGER FAR AWAY

Transport, hotels and travel agencies are the three pillars of the tourist industry. Any tour means going from one place to another, and that requires means of transport.

In the 1980s, China's transport industry remained a "bottleneck" for the development of its tourist industry. That is because, though the transport industry developed rapidly, the tourist industry grew at an even faster pace. The situation has changed in the 1990s. This has been due to good cooperation between tourist departments and departments providing air, railway, road and water transportation. It has also been due to a dramatic increase in transport facilities: the expansion of airports, railway stations and wharves; a big increase in the number of flights and the runs of trains, buses and ships; and the opening of new air, rail, highway and water routes. In the meantime, management has been improved, as has the quality of services. As a result, it has become more convenient and faster than ever for foreign tourists to come to China and travel from one place to another within the country.

It takes only eight hours for an aircraft to fly from

Stockholm in northern Europe to Beijing and no more than 12 – 14 hours for one to fly from western Europe, North America or Australia to Beijing. "Far-away China" has become a historical concept.

China used to have only one airline. It now has 25 airlines, a result of economic restructuring. Among them are six "key" airlines: Air China, China Eastern, China Southern, China Southwestern, China Northwestern and China Northern. The rest of them, 17 in all, are regional airlines: Xinjiang, General, Xiamen, Shanghai, Xinhua, Sichuan, Wuhan, Great Wall, Shenzhen, Hainan, Yunnan, Zhejiang, Nanjing, Fujian, Zhongyuan, Guizhou and Chang'an.

For years, about 70 percent of all China – bound foreign tourists came into the country by air. In recent years, the number of tourist arrivals has kept increasing. Though other means of transport have diverted part of the flow of passengers, the majority of tourists still come to

A sightseeing tour bus

China by air. At present, 94 international air routes link China with 53 cities in 30 countries and two regions in the world.

Domestic air routes now number 835, which link 112 cities. The number of civilian airports has increased to 139, which are located across

哥本哈根
COPENHAGEN
斯德哥尔摩
STOCKHOLM
莫斯科
MOSCOW
赤塔
CHITA
伦敦
LONDON
柏林
BERLIN
乌兰巴托
ULAN BATOR
AMSTERDAM 阿姆斯特丹
巴黎
PARIS
法兰克福
FRANKFURT
维也纳
VIENNA
基辅
KIEV
布鲁塞尔BRUSSELS
苏黎世
ZURICH
慕尼黑
MUNICH
布加勒斯特
BUCHAREST
北京
BEIJIN
马德里
MADRID
罗马
ROME
贝尔格莱德
BELGRADE
依斯坦布尔
ISTANBUL
QIN
特拉维夫
TELAVIV
开罗
CAIRO
科威特
KUWAIT
昆明
KUMMING
广州
GUANGZ
沙迦
SHARIAH
卡拉奇
KABACHI
迪拜
DUBAI
仰光
RANGOON
河内
HANO
曼谷
BANGKOK
亚的斯亚贝巴
ADDIS ABABA
新加坡
SINGAPO

the width and breadth of the country, from Heihe in Heilongjiang province, northeast China, to Sanya on the southern tip of Hainan Island, Kashi in the central Asian region of Xinjiang and Shanghai in east China.

China's civil aviation industry buys a considerable

Map of China's international air routes

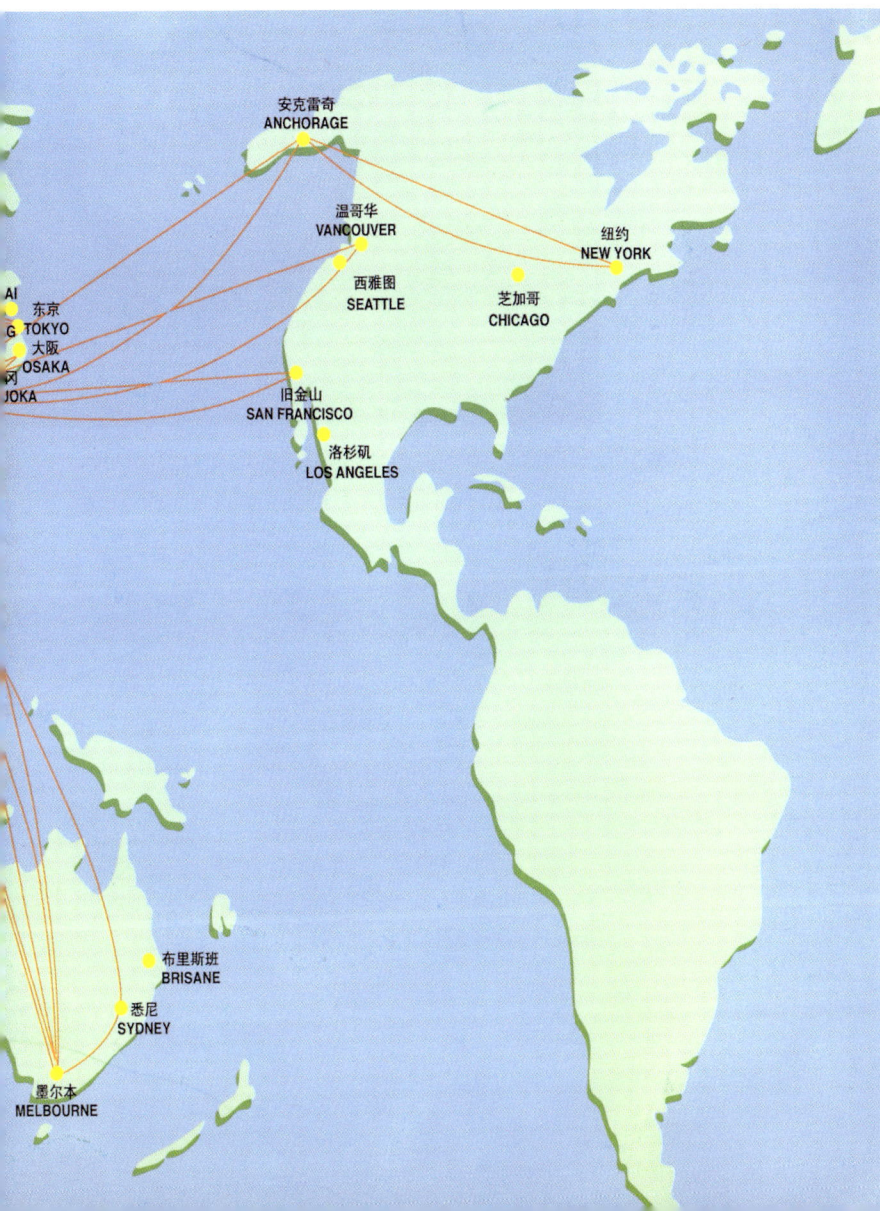

number of aircraft every year and its carrying capacity has increased by 20 – 30 percent annually in recent years. At present, it has a total of 416 aircraft, and the number keeps increasing at a rapid pace. Chinese airlines use long – range Boeing, McDonnell Douglas and Air – Bus aircraft for its international flights. On domestic routes, airlines use medium – and short – range Short, Fokker, BAE, Saab, Yak and home – made Yun – 7 aircraft, in addition to Boeings, McDonnell Douglases and Air Buses. The international aircraft manufacturing industry regards China as the biggest potential aircraft market in the world.

What China's civil aviation industry is most proud

of is that, for decades, it has kept an accident – free safety record for its international flights. Safety continues to be the industry's top priority.

China's civil aviation industry has joined the International Aviation Telecommunications Society. Through computers, it has automatic control over seat reservations on international flights, has instant access to information about the seating situation of major international airlines on its major air routes and is able to book seats on required flights for passengers.

Constant improvements have been made in services, too. Chinese airlines have sent air stewardesses abroad for training and exchanged air stewardesses with Japan Airlines as a way of improving their service standards. Shanghai Airline has recruited air stewardesses from among unemployed female textile workers. Called "air aunties," these middle – aged stewardesses have won praise from customers with their gentle manners and first – rate services.

Seven Chinese airlines have set up 67 offices abroad. Air China, the national carrier, has offices in the following 33 cities: Addis Ababa, Belgrade, Berlin, Bucharest, Cairo, Copenhagen, Frankfurt, Fukuoka, Hong Kong, Istanbul, Jakarta, Karachi, Kuwait, London, Melbourne, Moscow, Bangkok, New York, Osaka, Paris, Rome, San Francisco, Sharjah, Singapore, Stockholm, Sydney, Tokyo, Zurich, Toronto, Ulan Bator, Vancouver, Vienna and Yangoon. China Eastern Airline has 13 offices abroad: Tokyo, Fukuoka, Osaka, Nagoya, Nagasaki, Chicago, Seattle, Los Angeles, Bahrain,

Tour buses are easily available in Suzhou.

Brussels, Madrid, Seoul and Hong Kong. China Southern Airline has 11 offices abroad: Bangkok, Manila, Kuala Lumpur, Jakarta, Surabaya, Penang, Hanoi, Ho Chi Minh City, Vientiane, Seoul and Singapore. China Southwestern Airline has offices in Katmandu and Singapore. China Northern Airline has offices in Khabarovsk, Irkutsk, Pyongyang and Seoul. Xinjiang Airline has offices in Moscow and Alma – Ata. Yunnan Airline has offices in Yangoon and Singapore. They all provide consulting services for foreign tourists.

Trains play an important role in China's tourist industry. Foreign tourists like to choose the train as their means of transport for medium – and short – distance travels within China. That is because train rides provide the traveler with views on the way and access to ordinary Chinese.

China's railway network has some 60,000 km of track. It covers all provinces and regions ex-

克拉玛依KARAMAY

乌鲁木齐 ÜRÜMQI

阿克苏AKSU

喀什KASHI

和田HOTAN

敦煌DUNHUANG

银川

西宁XINING

兰州LA

拉萨LHASA

重庆

昆明KUNMING

cept Tibet.

Over the last decade, the Chinese Ministry of Railways has taken a series of measures to increase the rail network's carrying capacity. First,

海拉尔HAILAR

齐齐哈尔QIQIHAR

乌兰浩特ULANHOT 哈尔滨HARBIN

长春CHANGCHUN 吉林JILIN
锡林浩特XILINHOT
通辽TONGLIAO 延吉YANJI
赤峰CHIFENG
浩特HOHHOT 沈阳SHENYANG

北京BEIJING 秦皇岛QINHUANGDAO

天津TIANJIN 大连DALIAN

YUAN 烟台YANTAI
石家庄SHIJIAZHUANG
青岛QINGDAO
济南JINAN
AN
郑州ZHENGZHOU
UOYANG
徐州XUZHOU

南京NANJING 南通NANTONG
GFAN 合肥HEFEI 常州CHANGZHOU 上海SHANGHAI
武汉WUHAN 杭州HANGZHOU
宁波NINGBO
NGJIAJIE 黄山HUANGSHAN
南昌NANCHANG 温州WENZHOU
CHANGSHA
福州FUZHOU
台北TAIPEI
夏门XIAMEN
GUANGZHOU 汕头SHANTOU
珠ZHUHAI 深圳SHENZHEN
澳门MACAO 香港HONGKONG
湛江ZHANJIANG
海口HAIKOU
亚SANYA

南海诸岛
SOUTH CHINA
SEA ISLANDS

to build new lines. In 1996, for example, the 2,536
- km Beijing - Kowloon Railway was completed
and open to traffic, providing a basic condition
for the development of tourist resources along the

China Is No Longer Far Away 113

way. Second, to double – track and electrify important lines. Third, to hitch extra cars onto trains running on tourist routes to increase seating capacity. Fourth, to run special tourist trains on hot tour routes: Beijing – Badaling section of the Great Wall, Nanchang – Jiujiang, Shanghai – Hangzhou, Beijing – Qinhuangdao, Beijing – Chengde, and Qingdao – Tai'an. Fifth, to increase the speed of trains. Trains now run at 140km/h, for example, on the Guangzhou – Kowloon, Shanghai – Nanjing and Beijing – Beidaihe routes,

The Sichuan-Tibet Highway, whose average elevation exceeds 3,000 meters above the sea level, is the highest in the world altitudinally.

The Jiujiang Bridge across the Yangtze

more than double the original speed. And Sixth, to renovate or expand railway stations in important tourist cities to allow great passenger flow. These stations serve Guilin, Xi'an, Shanghai, Suzhou, Beidaihe, Chengde, Xiamen and Tianjin. In Beijing, a new railway station, Beijing West, was built.

Twelve pairs of trains running on major tour routes have been equipped with closed – circuit TV systems showing programs on resorts, places of historical interest and folk customs as well as entertainment programs. Trains running between Beijing and Qingdao have a night bar; and those running on the Guangzhou – Shenzhen route offer self – served meals.

In cooperation with railway operators, tour providers arrange ad hoc express tour trains for foreign tourists in China. Train routes are decided by foreign tour groups; trains stop while their passengers are sightseeing; and they run while their passengers are sleeping. Take for example, a train running eastward along the ancient Silk Road: it starts at Shihezi in the central Asian region of Xinjiang, stops at Turpan, Dunhuang and Jiayuguan Pass of the Great Wall on the way, and ends at Xi'an. The luxury international tour express, "the Oriental Express," running from north to south after entering China, stops at a host of Chinese cities to allow passengers to see sights. It then goes to Hong Kong and Japan.

Travel by bus has advantages over that by air and train since buses provide "door – to – door" services. And travel by bus does not suffer inconveniences that come with travel by other means such as changes and waiting at airports or railway stations. In recent years, China has made remarkable progress in highway construction. That is why an increasing number of tourists go by bus on medium – and short – distance trips.

"Want to get rich ? Build roads." This has been a popular saying in China since economic reform began almost two decades ago. People have realized the close relationship between good transport conditions and economic prosperity. The tourist industry has benefited from this awakening. At present, highways open to motor traffic throughout the country reach more than 1.21 million km in length. In some provinces and municipalities in east China, highways link almost

Taxis are easily available in cities across China.

A flyover in Beijing

all villages and townships. Even remote areas are now accessible by highways.

Expressways have been built between important tourist cities. Pairs or groups of cities linked by expressways include: Beijing – Tianjin, Shenyang – Dalian, Shenzhen – Guangzhou – Zhuhai, Chengdu – Chongqing, Shanghai – Nanjing, Shanghai – Hangzhou, Jinan – Qingdao, Luoyang – Kaifeng, Xi'an – Lintong and Hefei – Nanjing. The time of travel between these cities has been cut by one half or two thirds. Some roads have been built especially for tourism such as Guilin – Yangshuo, Guangzhou – Zhaoqing, Tai'an – Qufu, Zhengzhou – Kaifeng and Chengdu – Guanxian County.

Construction of expressways is being accelerated in China. By the end of this century, the

The Banda Airport in Qamdo, Tibet – so far the world's highest airport altitudinally

country will have two north – south and two east – west expressways traversing its entire length and breadth.

Tourist motor vehicle companies in China have a total of 21,544 tourist buses and cars, of which most are imports bearing Mercedes, Hino, Nissan, Toyota, Chevrolet and Citroen brands. There are also Audis and Santanas made by Sino – foreign joint ventures in China. These buses and cars are fast and air – conditioned. Some long – distance buses are each equipped with televisions, a refrigerator and a toilet. The Greyhound bus company of the United States now operates on the Shanghai – Nanjing Expressway.

Public transportation in cities is going three – dimensional. The taxi business is well developed in all cities, big and small. Elevated roads have been built in Beijing, Guangzhou and Shanghai. Beijing had its first subway in 1969 and is now served by two lines. Shanghai and Tianjin have each built a subway in recent years. Guangzhou and Chengdu are planning to build one each. In Shanghai, the number of cross – Huangpu tunnels has increased to four.

It is a pleasure to have a cruise on rivers, lakes and the sea. International passenger ships call regularly at the Chinese ports of Dalian, Tianjin (Tanggu), Qingdao, Yantai, Weihai, Shanghai, Xiamen, Shenzhen and Haikou. Luxury cruise ships from Britain, France, Greece, the United States and Russia also call at these ports. Of China's foreign tourists in 1995, 16.3 percent came to the country by water.

A total of 248 ships operated by tour – transport companies cruise on the Three Gorges section of the Yangtze, Lijiang river at Guilin, the Grand Canal, Taihu Lake, FuchunJiang river, the

The snow-capped Kangrin Boqi

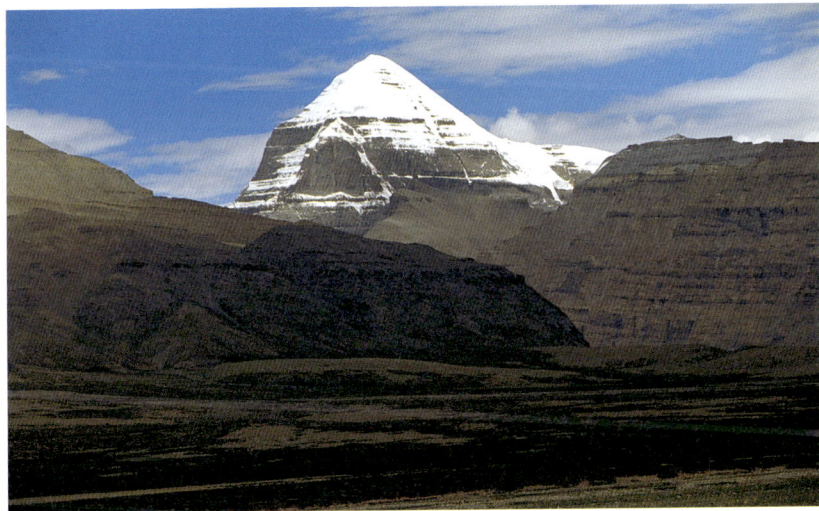

Thousand – Island Lake, the Pearl river, Songhua river and the Yellow River. Most of these ships are well equipped.

Companies operating ships, trains and buses offer through transport services. Tour routes where such services are available include Beijing – Qingdao – Yantai, Beijing – Dalian, Guangzhou – Zhongshan, Wuhan – Mount Lushan, Chengdu – Chongqing – Yichang, and Beijing – Mount Taishan.

China's telecom industry has made rapid progress in the last decade and more. A well – developed telcom network links China with the rest of the world via cable, satellite and microwave. Tourists in all major Chinese cities have easy access to direct – dial international telephones. Rooms in all three – star and more upscale hotels are equipped with digitally – transmitted telephones. A national information network that has gradually taken shape since the early 1980s enables most travel agencies and tourist hotels to have instant access to business – related information and to book rooms and air tickets for tourists.

In 1997, China National Tourism Administration established a China Tourism Net through CHINANET of the Chinese Ministry of Posts and Telecommunications (changed to Ministry of Information Industry in early 1998) and the INTERNET. The first phase of the project covers 28 provinces and autonomous regions, four centrally – adminis-

The Bixia (Blue-Cloud) Temple on Mount Taishan built in the Song Dynasty

tered municipalities and the Hong Kong Special Administrative Region. Tourism – related information available on the net amounts to more than four million words with indexes in both English and Chinese. Information covers tourist attractions, tour routes, tourist hotels and restaurants, special tours, tourist themes, shopping, folk customs and lifestyles, holidays, places of entertainment, performances, foreign – bound tours, relevant government regulations, tourist news dispatches and tourist organizations. China Tourism Net also has the functions of sending E – mail, transmitting official notices and replying to inquiries about tourism – related information, among others. The Web site of China Tourism Net is:

http://www.cnta.com

INTERNATIONAL SOURCE MARKETS: GOING STEADY

China's open – door policy formulated and adopted in the late 1970s marked its entry into the international tourist market. For the previous three decades, the country had shut itself up from the rest of the world, creating a sense of mystery in the mind of many foreigners. Once its doors were thrown open, the curious poured into China to see what it was like.

The first post – opening decade saw a dramatic increase in the number of China – bound foreign tourists. In 1988 the number of tourist arrivals from overseas was more than 36 times that in 1979. During this ten – year period, annual increase in tourist arrivals averaged 25 percent, a rate of growth not seen elsewhere on the world tourist market.

During 1979 – 1988, the biggest source of international customers for China's tourist industry was Japan and the United States. Each year, Japanese tourists accounted for one third of all foreign tourist arrivals and American tourists one fifth. Japanese and Americans together made up more than half of all China – bound international tourists.

The second biggest source was France, Britain

and West Germany. People from these countries made up 12 percent of all tourist arrivals in China.

Other major sources were Singapore, Thailand and the Philippines (11 – 12 percent) and Australia and Canada (10 – 12 percent).

The above – mentioned ten countries – Japan, the United States, France, Britain, West Germany, Singapore, Thailand, the Philippines, Australia and Canada – supplied more than 85 percent of all China – bound tourists. They were the 10 biggest customer sources for China's tourist industry in the 1980s. Among them, four are Asian countries.

In 1989, the international business of China's tourist industry plummeted. In less than two years, the market for China – bound tours revived. The industry then had some new customer

Some foreign tourists like to observe religious ceremonies.

sources, mainly Malaysia, Indonesia, the Republic of Korea, Mongolia and Russia. A new market structure has thus emerged.

By the end of 1996, countries where originated the biggest number of China – bound tourists were, in descending order, Japan, the Republic of Korea, the United States, Russia, Malaysia, Singapore, Mongolia, the Philippines, Britain, Thailand, Germany, Canada, Indonesia, Australia and France. Among them are eight Asian countries, which, together with Russia, make up 60 percent of these countries. That is to say, more than half of them are China's neighbors. This is a common pattern for the tourist industries of most countries in the world. That is because tours originating in neighboring countries cover short distances, cost less and are less prone to disruption by unexpected events in the world. However, Europe and North America are indisputably the most important customer sources for the world's tourist industry. China will not ne-

Watching a night performance in Wang Shi Yuan, a classic garden in Suzhou

Dancing in the
Stone Forest in
Yunnan Province

glect these markets.

In 1997, tourist arrivals from overseas reached 57.59 million, up 12.64 percent over the previous year. Arrivals with at least one – night stay in China reached 23.77 million, up 4.41 percent over the previous year, to maintain the sixth place in the world. In terms of tourist arrivals, China's share in global tourism went up to 3.85 percent in 1997, from 2.3 percent in 1990.

In 1997, tourist arrivals from foreign countries reached 7.428 million, up 10.14 percent over the previous year and 3.17 percent over the planned number. The country's tourist industry reported revenues of US$12.074 billion in foreign exchange, up 18.37 percent over the previous year and in excess of planned earnings by 9.76 percent. In terms of earnings, China's tourist industry ranked eighth in 1997, from ninth in the previous year, and its share in the global tourist industry increased to 2.69 percent, from 0.82 percent in 1990.

Judged from the trend of development, China's tourist industry is not likely to enjoy again double – digit growth either in the number of arrivals or in revenues. With regard to its international markets, high growth is expected to give way to a slow but steady development. In the year 2000, according to an estimate by the National Tourism Administration, tourist arrivals from abroad are expected to reach 8.2 – 8.6 million, or 54.5 – 55 million if day trippers from Hong Kong and Macao are included; and revenues of the industry are expected to reach US$14 billion.

China – bound tourists differ in cultural background and value perceptions. Viewed from their existing and potential psychological requirements, they have the following characteristics:

More individualistic in taste. Tourists in the present era have increasingly greater expecta-

Sampling Peking roast duck is a must while in Beijing.

tions from their tours. They are not satisfied with ordinary tourist products. Rather, they seek self – fulfillment and self – improvement through tours. When they come to China, they would like to gain special life experiences by visiting some places visited by few people.

A trend among foreign tourists in China has been to disperse widely, for a wide range of tour routes and destinations. No longer are they concentrated in a few cities. Rather, an increasing number of tourists visit less familiar places in the heart or remote parts of the country. The hottest tour route for people from Europe and North America used to be Beijing, Shanghai, Xi'an and Guilin. Guangzhou would be another city on the "golden route" if they entered and left China via Hong Kong. In recent years, however, with the exception of Beijing, these cities have seen an occasional drop in the number of European and North American tourists as patrons. On the other hand, there has been a dramatic increase in the number of tourists visiting formerly less popular cities such as Tianjin, Hefei, Wenzhou, Changsha and Weihai.

Owing to the fact that tourists differ in culture, occupation, age and interest, strong individuality on the part of tourists requires that the tourist industry provide special tours and special – interest tourist products. Tourism is a kind of

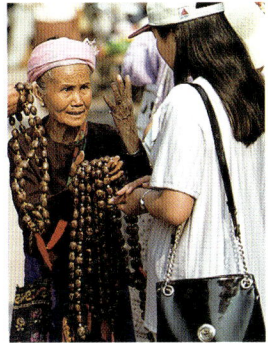

Even Grandma has learned to sell a thing or two to tourists.

cultural consumption. Along with a higher level of cultural attainment on the part of tourists, tourist products need to have an increasingly richer cultural content. Back – to – nature tours and tours allowing tourists to understand a reforming and opening China are quite popular.

On their own. International tourists in the present era are mature. Touring different countries in the world and rich in experience, they have great self – confidence in having long – distance tours on their own. They have strong adaptability. For some, language barrier is a welcome challenge rather than a deterrent. In short, there has been an increasing number of individual tourists who would like to come and go on their own. For them, being a member of a tour group deprives them of freedom. As a result, recent years have seen a marked increase in the number of individual tourists coming to China.

Since there will always be tourists going abroad for the first time and tourists of an advanced age,

Looking for the source of the Yangtze River in the Tanggula Range in northwest China

Homes of Bai fishermen at Erhai Lake in Yunnan Province

group tours will not disappear altogether. But an irresistible trend is the decline of group tours and a continued increase in the number of individual tourists. Many tourists do not like pre – designed and pre – packaged existing tourist products. They would rather select routes and combine products on their own. The widespread use of computers, in particular, has helped the trend. Some tourists book air tickets and room reservations directly from airlines and hotels by computers, bypassing travel agencies. As a result, travel agencies are beginning to change their business strategies: to provide "supermarket" service for individual travelers, that is to say, let tourists choose service items themselves and help them design and package tourist products in accordance with their wishes.

Experience. For international tourists, the pur-

A Tibetan Opera performance

pose of traveling abroad is to enrich their experiences. Buying a tourist product is buying a life experience. That is why they like to stay longer in one or two places instead of rushing from one place to another according to a "whirlwind" schedule.

Tourists want not only to see but also to participate in activities. That is why they like participatory tour programs such as "Be a Shanghai Citizen for a Day," "Be a Guest in a Beijing Courtyard Home" and "Making a Porcelain Bowl in Jingdezhen, the Porcelain Capital."

Frequent Travels. For many people, traveling has become a way of life, a routine in life. People nowadays travel once or several times every year instead of once every few years, as was the case in the past. With an increase in traveling frequency, tourists spend less time and visit fewer places on each trip.

Owing to the fact that travel has become more or less a routine affair, tourists are more casual in the way they make preparations. Travelers used to book reservations with travel agencies one year or half a year in advance, but now they do that one month, half a month, or even a week in advance, and often change their schedule after making reservations. Travel agencies are making operational adjustments to adapt to such changes.

What a foreign tourist needs to do if he or she would like to visit Tibet:

Passport and visa: a foreign tourist wishing to go to Tibet must have a passport issued by the government of his or her country and a visa issued by a Chinese embassy abroad; a visa is not necessary if his or her country has signed a visa-abolition agreement with China.

Tibet-entry confirmation notice: an organized foreign tour group wishing to go to Tibet must entrust the Tibet Travel Agency to apply for and obtain a Tibet-entry confirmation notice on its behalf; the Tibet Tourism Administration also has offices in Beijing, Chengdu and Qinghai's Golmud, which provide consulting services on Tibet tour-related matters for individual tourists.

Weather conditions, what to wear: spring (March-May): cold, extremely windy, dry; jacket and woolen sweater; summer (June-August): cool, fairly hot at noon; thin and light wear; autumn (September-November): fairly cold, dry; jacket and woolen sweater; winter (December-February): cold, extremely dry; light but warm clothes.

Air travel: Chengdu-Lhasa; Beijing-Chengdu-Lhasa; Chongqing-Lhasa; Kathmandu (Nepal)-Lhasa.

DOMESTIC TOURISM
– A HUGE MARKET

Rapid economic development in China has changed the spending habit and lifestyle of the Chinese people. With more leisure time after the introduction of the five – work – day week in 1995 as well as more income, an increasing number of Chinese have taken an interest in travels. This has given rise to a national tourism fever.

The most striking change that has taken place on China's tourist market since the beginning of the 1990s is a rapid development of domestic tourism. Business volume was 644 million person/times in 1997, generating revenues of 211.27 billion yuan (US$25.45 billion), up 28.95 percent over the previous year and in excess of planned earnings for the year by 17.4 percent.

Domestic tourists make up 94 percent of all tourists in China and revenues of the domestic tourist business account for 64 percent of the total revenues of the country's tourist industry as a whole. That is to say, the domestic tourist business is a vital part of China's tourist industry.

According to an analysis by economists, of urban households in China at present, 34 percent are of a have – enough – to – eat type, 55 percent lead a fairly comfortable life, and 7 percent are of a well – off type. That is to say, most families have the financial ability to go on sightseeing tours within the country.

More and more Chinese families are no longer worried about food and clothing. Their housing conditions have also kept improving. And most have bought almost all kinds of home appliances they need. They now naturally turn to travel as a way to improve the quality of their life. Introduction of the double – day weekend has fueled the travel fervor among the Chinese.

According to a sample survey, tour – related

A weekend excursion to Beijing's hilly suburbs

spending accounts for 10 percent of a family's total expenditures in Beijing and 11 percent in Shanghai; for self – paying tours, daily average spending is 200 yuan for a Guangdonger, 150 yuan for a Shanghai traveler and 120 yuan for a Beijinger.

At a time when China is developing a market economy, an increasing number of people go on sightseeing tours, spend holidays away from their homes, make business trips, and travel to different places to attend meetings, look for jobs or visit friends and relatives. Never has the Chinese nation been as actively on the move as it is now.

Regional disparities in economic development

has prompted young people to leave their hometowns in underdeveloped areas to seek jobs elsewhere in the country. In recent years job – seeking boys and girls have swelled into torrents. Before these new migrants have settled down in their adopted places, they travel frequently to their hometowns for home visits.

In economically developed areas in southern China, some enterprises have begun giving employees free tours as a reward for good performance and to nurture loyalty.

What merits attention is that, of all domestic tourists, 60 percent are from the countryside. Chinese peasants, tied to the land for thousands

The Summer Palace in Beijing, which combines natural with cultural sights, is a representative product of oriental gardening.

of years, have developed an urge to travel now that an increasing number of them have the financial ability to do so. This is a market with more than 800 million potential customers. Many farmer – employees working in rural enterprises in well – off areas of Guangdong have been to Beijing on sightseeing tours. They went there and back by air and stayed in three – star hotels in the capital.

Most Chinese travel for sightseeing, but recent years have seen a demand for vacationing tours. It reflects a desire to leave concrete – and – steel office buildings in cities and live for a while amid green trees and grass. Back – to – nature is mankind's "recessive atavism," as some people say.

Most Chinese families have kept the tradition of respecting the old and caring for the young. China's population of retirees has kept increas-

The Apakhoja Tomb in Kashgar, Xinjiang

Chengde Mountain Resort in Hebei Province, built in the 18th century as summer residence for Qing emperors.

ing in size. With financial support from their children as well as pension, a considerable number of retirees can afford to take sightseeing travels and, in recent years, an increasing number of them have actually joined the army of tourists. Chinese parents are only too willing to invest in the future of their only child. As a result, there has been an increase in the number of study tours, summer camps and winter camps for children and youngsters.

According to an estimate by the China National Tourism Administration, by the year 2000, the domestic tour business will exceed one billion person/times and its revenues will reach 250 – 260 billion yuan(US$30.12 – 31.33 billion) .

While China is welcoming foreign tourists, an increasing number of Chinese are visiting foreign countries as tourists. The number of such Chinese was 2.93 million in 1992, 3.74 million in 1993, 3.73 million in 1994, 4.71 million in 1995, 5.06 million in 1996, and 5.32 million in 1997. Some countries in Southeast Asia and Oceania have listed China as a big potential customer - source market for their tourist industries.

However, 5.32 million people account for only 0.4 percent of the Chinese population. Even if the number of Chinese going abroad for sightseeing tours increases to 10 million annually in a few years, that still accounts for less than 1 percent of the national population. That is to say, for 99 percent of the Chinese people, destinations for their leisure tours are still within the country. That is why some theme parks featuring foreign sights have attracted large numbers of tourists in recent years.

Of Beijingers who on weekends visit Tianjin 120 km away, 15 percent drive their own cars.

The Penglai Pavilion in Shandong Province

A time-honored wind-and-rain bridge in Guizhou, southwest China.

Private ownership of cars was unthinkable in China a few years ago but is a hot topic today. According to a survey, the number of Chinese families having the financial ability to buy a car at present is about 6 million, 2 percent of the total. However, there are only a little more than 2 million private cars throughout the country. According to a forecast by the State Development Planning Commission, the time when large numbers of cars begin entering Chinese homes is 2010. It is expected that the development of private cars will inevitably change people's spending habit and mode of traveling, including the content, ways and radius of travels and the structure and level of travel – related spending. By then, Beijingers will drive to Chengde and Beidaihe for holidays and people in Shanghai drive to Suzhou and Hangzhou for weekends.

RADIATING EFFECTS OF THE TOURIST INDUSTRY

If "Do you favor the development of a tourist industry?" is a question in an opinion poll conducted in Chinese cities today, almost all would answer "yes." If you ask local officials the question "What's the good of developing a tourist industry?" most of them would enumerate benefits the industry would bring to the local economy and people's life.

China's international tourist industry, with revenues exceeding the US$10 billion mark in 1996 and reaching US$12 billion in 1997, now ranks among the world's biggest tour providers. Its domestic tourist business has annual revenues of more than 100 billion yuan and keeps growing. In 1997, revenues exceeded 200 billion yuan. These are direct, obvious benefits of the tourist industry. On the other hand, tourism is a comprehensive industry with a strong penetrating and rippling effect. It brings indirect benefits that can be many times bigger than direct benefits — recessive effects in economic, social and environmental fields.

In the past decade and more, the Chinese have gradually come to understand the role of the tourist industry.

Reform and opening have promoted the development of the tourist industry. This is true conversely: the development of a tourist industry has helped the implementation of reform and opening policies in greater depth and width.

The tourist industry is a window for reform and opening up and an important channel for China's international contacts and exchanges. Tours mean the flow of people, and the flow of people generates the flow of capital, of goods, of information and of science and technology.

Weifang in Shandong is a small emerging industrial city. By chance, the president of the kite as-

Mount Wutai in Shanxi Province – a Buddhist shrine

Scriptural streamers and Mani Piles by the Namco Lake in Tibet are a form of prayer for happiness.

sociation in Seattle, the United States, found that kites made locally in traditional ways are extremely beautiful and exquisite and organized successive American groups for kite – flying tours in Weifang. That has led to the annual Weifang International Kite Festival attended by more than 20 countries and over 20 Chinese provinces. The kite festivals have gradually become trade fairs where economic and trade information is exchanged and trade deals worth billions of yuan are done annually. These have promoted not only the development of Weifang's tourist industry and retail business but also economic development in the six surrounding counties.

In Hebei province's Laishui county, 200 km from Beijing, is a hilly area called Yeshanpo (literally "Wild Hill Slopes"). It used to be extremely poor. Beginning from the mid – 1980s, the county began developing a tourist industry by making use of wilderness – flavored sights in the area. Tourists began visiting the area in growing numbers. And this has prompted local farmers to open family inns and restaurants, treat tourists to local produce and home – made food, and provide other services to tourists such as horse rides and photography. More than 3,000 locals are directly involved in the tourist industry. Six townships with a total of 27 villages have benefited from the tourist industry. The farmers have become well – off, as a result. Many families have built new houses and bought new furniture. Some farmers installed modern sanitary facilities in their homes. Ownership of television sets has increased dramatically. In fact, Yeshanpo has become the

The Longmen Grottoes near Luoyang, Henan Province, dating back to the fifth century. The statue of Buddha is a masterpiece of stone sculpture.

first "TV Village" — one set at least for each household — in the entire Taihang mountainous region.

Near Xi'an, Xiahe Village where the Qin Emperor Mausoleum is located used to be as poor as Hebei's Yeshanpo. Tourists have kept pouring to the place since the Qin Emperor's terra - cotta soldiers and horses were unearthed and displayed. The villagers make miniature replicas of Qin soldiers and horses as well as handicraft articles characteristic of Qin culture such as embroidered pieces, pillow cases, jackets and tiger - headed shoes and sell them to tourists. Eighty percent of the village's labor force is engaged in business. A village - run language class teaches farmers English. Women villagers in their sixties or seventies can haggle prices with foreign tourists in simple English. The villagers have become well - off and are better informed about the outside world.

The above are just a few examples. In fact, such

The making of tourist souvenirs has stimulated economic development in areas inhabited by ethnic minority people.

A bazaar in Kashgar, Xinjiang

stories are repeated wherever tourism is thriving as an industry. Some counties and townships are developing tourist industry as a "pillar" of their respective economies. In economically underdeveloped areas and areas inhabited by ethnic minority peoples, some local governments have decided to develop tourist industry as an important strategic measure to eliminate local poverty.

Tourism has not only enriched villages and counties but also changed the fate of some professions and trades.

The making of tri – colored glazed pottery dates back to the Tang Dynasty more than 1,000 years ago. Luoyang city in Henan province used to be the production center for such pottery, but the industry there later declined and seemed to

Flying kites during the Weifang International Kite-Flying Festival

Inside a Western-style restaurant

have no future. Tourism has saved the industry. Glazed ceramic horses and camels made in the Tang tri – colored style are popular souvenirs for domestic and foreign tourists alike. With tourists as unconscious promoters, they are exported to more than 40 countries and regions in the world. The number of factories making Tang – style tri – colored ceramic artifacts in the city has increased to 200 and their annual output value reaches tens of millions of yuan.

New year pictures and watercolor block – printed pictures are traditional handicrafts of Tianjin's Yangliuqing. It is tourism again that has saved the folk art from going into oblivion and made it flourish. Benefiting from tourism in varying degrees are industries making earthen pots (Nixing, Jiangsu), jade cups (Jiuquan, Gansu), cloisonne ware (Beijing) and inkslabs (Shexian, Anhui).

China's food culture promotes the develop-

ment of tourism, and tourism in turn compels the catering industry to keep improving itself. Tourism encourages restaurants to compete against, and learn from, one another and promotes exchanges between various cooking schools. For example, dishes of different cuisines are mutually adopted, and well – known chefs, invited by high – paying restaurants and hotels at home and abroad, have been able to demonstrate their skills in different cities. Tourism has also given rise to classes offering professional training on tourism – oriented cooking and to tourism-oriented cooking contests. All these have enabled China's catering industry to keep scaling new heights.

Tourism has saved some well – known traditional dinners from going into oblivion such as man han quan xi (Manchu – Han All – Course Dinner). Efforts involved include the study of relevant historical records and learning from retired famous chefs. Traditional feasts that have been

The Qinhuai River in Nanjing

revived in recent years to attract tourists include a palace - style dinner, a Confucian Family - style dinner, an aristocrat-style dinner as described in "Dream of the Red Mansions," a classic novel written in the mid - Qing Dynasty, and a monastery - style vegetarian dinner.

Recent years have seen the influx into China of catering businesses from Europe, North America and other Asian countries. All star - rated hotels in China have Western - style restaurants. Well - known Western fast food chains such as Mcdonald's, Kentucky Fried Chicken and Pizza Hut have opened numerous outlets in Chinese cities. All these have provided conveniences for foreign tourists and enriched China's food and drinks market as well.

The tourist industry has a strong rippling effect. In China, it promotes the development of more than 20 economic sectors including: light and textile industries, agriculture, animal husbandry, fisheries, commerce, banking, insurance, civil aviation, rail transport, water transport, posts and telecom, building materials, construction, real estate, gardening, museums, hotel business, catering, handicraft industry, entertainment, advertisement and health care.

According to a survey in Shanghai, the proportions of tourism – sourced income in total income for different trades are: 90 percent for hotels, 85 percent for the transportation industry, 50 percent for the catering industry, 25 percent for posts and telecom, 20 – 30 percent for parks and cultural facilities, 10 percent for commerce, and 2 percent for banking and insurance. Every yuan in income for the tourist industry generates about 5 yuan for other related sectors.

By the end of 1996, a total of 1.197 million people in China were engaged in international tourism. They refer to people working in hotels, travel agencies, transport companies and commercial outlets that serve foreign tourists as well as those working in tourism administrations. According to a report on the international tourist industry, a job in the tourist industry generally means five jobs in other related sectors. Calcu-

Scenery in the Altai range in northern Xinjiang

Wild donkeys in
northern Tibet

lated in this way, more than 6 million people in
China are engaged, directly or indirectly, in the
country's international tourist industry. In addition, there are more people serving domestic tourists. Worldwide, the tourist industry employs, directly and indirectly, 11 percent of total labor
force on average. It is expected that in China this
proportion will be soon reached and exceeded.

Many businessmen and investors from overseas
often come to China first as tourists. As tourists,
they try to understand China's policies on foreign
investment, investigate the investment environment and seek potential partners for cooperation
—   preparations prior to actually investing in the
country. The Sino – Japanese Friendship Water
Plant in Changchun, northeast China, for example, has been built with Japanese capital that
came through a tourism – opened channel. There
are many similar examples across the country.

Among China – bound tourists are high – ranking officials as well as ordinary people. There are also numerous professionals dedicated to science and technology, education, culture, the arts and sports. They bring to China the latest information and, at the same time, help spread Chinese culture.

China's scientific research institutes, institutions of higher learning, hospitals, sports organizations and environmental protection agencies often receive foreign tour groups from corresponding fields. Aside from visiting and doing investigations, these tour groups often hold seminars and academic exchanges with their Chinese counterparts. Some Chinese academic organizations sometimes receive books and equipment from their foreign guests as gifts. Examples: a foreign educational tour group gave a Chinese university thousands of technical books after paying it a

A wild giant panda

Siberian red-billed cranes migrate to Kunming, Yunnan, for the winter.

visit; a foreign tour group consisting of gynecologists gave a Chinese hospital a sophisticated medical machine as a gift after paying it a visit.

Among special tour groups received by China International Travel Service are those interested respectively in shadow boxing, qigong (deep – breathing exercises), acupuncture anesthesia, tea cultivation and earthquake forecast. Their visits have promoted Sino – foreign exchanges in cultural and scientific fields.

While traveling around China, foreign tour groups also try to know China's socialist system, its political, economic, military, cultural and educational aspects, its economic reforms, and the results of its open policy. Many tourists say they have acquired a better understanding of issues. One such issue is China's family planning policy. After visiting kindergartens, nurseries and Chinese families, they have come to realize that, rather than a unique Chinese problem, excessive population growth is a difficult problem faced by the world as a whole, and that it is necessary for China to apply a family planning policy.

Tourism is an important factor contributing to urban construction. In cities, big and small, where tourists go, new buildings, roads and greenery keep adding to cityscapes; museums, libraries, gymnasiums and theaters have been renovated; many new facilities have been built such as dance

Golden monkey, a rare animal living in the primeval forests of southwest China

Sedimentation of calcium carbonate in the Huanglong scenic area in Sichuan Province – a very rare phenomenon in the world

halls, coffee shops, restaurants, bowling alleys, billiard rooms, skating rinks and golf courses; and neon lights keep increasing to make city nights ever brighter. All these are partly for tourists. In big cities such as Beijing and Shanghai, there are outdoor concerts on weekends; and vacation homes and entertainment facilities have been built in their suburbs.

As a result, the quality of life for China's urban residents has improved. They are able to make leisure travels, vacation away from their homes and otherwise enjoy themselves the way their ancestors could not even dream about.

"Tourism promotes development" is a slogan of the World Tourism Organization (WTO). This has been amply verified in China.

PROSPECTS OF CHINA'S TOURIST INDUSTRY

The tourist industry is likely to have the following characteristics in the 21st century:

—   Traveling for pleasure is expected to become a life necessity for more people and tends to be more frequent for each individual. The number of people making leisure tours worldwide is expected to increase from 702 million in the year 2000 to 1.018 billion in 2010; and the number of Chinese traveling for pleasure within the country to increase from 1 billion in the year 2000 to 2 - 2.5 billion in 2010.

—   With regard to the main activities of China - bound tourists, there is going to be a gradual shift from sightseeing to sightseeing plus vacationing. Gradually, there will be foreign tourists who visit China purely for vacationing. For domestic tourists, the shift from pure sightseeing to sightseeing plus vacationing is likely to be quicker than expected; weekend leisure activities are expected to develop into short vacations.

—   Ecology tourism, "back to nature," will become fashionable. People will show a stronger desire to visit forests, rivers, lakes, mountainous areas and villages.

— Stronger individuality on the part of tourists will compel the tourist trade to offer more products; more tourists are expected to travel along unbeaten tracks; and tourists will be much more dispersed geographically than before.

— Competition on the tourist market is expected to shift from that on prices to that on the cultural taste of tourist products, the quality of services, promotional effect, safety guarantees and business operation.

Given changes on the international and domestic tourist markets in the 21st century, China's tourist industry faces both opportunities and challenges.

The last two decades of the 20th century have witnessed a dramatic rise of a tourist industry in

The Jinshitan seaside resort in Dalian, Liaoning Province.

China. Tourist resources have been developed on a fairly big scale, but they still constitute a small proportion in the vast country; and furthermore, their geographical distribution is extremely uneven. From coastal to hinterland areas and from the south to the north, developed tourist resources decrease in density. In most parts of northeast and northwest China and in parts of

southwest and central China, developed tourist resources are mostly scattered rather than concentrated geographically, and numerous tracts of virgin land await development. Primeval forests, high mountains, deep ravines, deserts and folk customs in these areas are where China's potential to satisfy the tourist market in the 21st century lies. As a national strategy, economic devel-

Hong Kong remains a tourist center in the Asia-Pacific Region after its return to China.

opment will accelerate in the central and western regions of China in years to come. The tourist industry is expected to move in the same direction. This means that tourist resources in the country's hinterland will be developed in sync with its economic development or "appropriately in advance."

In the structure of China's tourist products, the dominance of sightseeing products will gradually give way to dominance by "sightseeing – vacationing" products. The industry will also develop purely vacationing products.

The following 12 state – level vacationing areas, under preparation since October 1992, now have the conditions to receive international and domestic vacationers: Jinshitang (Dalian), Shilaoren (Qingdao), Taihu Lake (Suzhou), Mount Mashan (Wuxi), Mount Sheshan (Shanghai), Zhijiang (Hangzhou), Mount Wuyi (Fujian), Meizhou Island (Fujian), Nanhu Lake (Guangzhou), the Silver Beach (Beihai), Haigeng (Kunming), and Yalong Bay (Sanya, Hainan). Dozens of provincial – level vacation areas have also been completed during the period and are ready to receive vacationers.

The tourist industry will continue to develop unique Chinese products, reach international standards in accommodation facilities and service quality, gradually link itself to the international information super highway, and pay even greater attention to the safety of tourists.

China's tourist industry in the 21st century will face two major challenges: competition from outside and environmental protection at home.

Growing competition comes from China's neighboring countries and regions where the tourist trade has kept developing at a fast pace. China must adopt ingenious and flexible marketing strategies to win market shares. It should also combine competition with cooperation.

Shanghai, a prosperous metropolis

More difficult will be the protection of ecology and environment. Tourism has been regarded as a "rising industry" in the 20th century. As it enters the 21st century, whether or not it will continue to have that reputation and whether or not its development will be sustainable lies in whether or not countries in the world can protect and improve their ecology and environment. This is certainly true, too, of China's tourist industry.

On this issue, China will adopt the policy of "development amid protection and protection amid development." For ecology tour areas, greater attention will be paid to the quality of tourists than to the number of visitors; and equal attention will be paid to ecological, economic and social effects.

Developed transportation boosts tourism, but a high density of tourists threatens ecology and environment. It is, therefore, necessary to continue improving transportation on the one hand and make sure that ecology tour areas are properly separated geographically from traffic arteries.

Tourism is a sensitive, fragile trade. Political upheavals, economic depression, armed conflicts, terrorist attacks, natural disasters and epidemics can all adversely affect or even bring to a stop the development of tourism. China will enhance its tourist industry's ability to meet emergencies on the one hand and strive to safeguard world

The Fuchunjiang
River in early spring

peace and stability together with other countries
on the other.

China hopes to have one of the most developed
tourist industries in the world at the beginning
of the 21st century. This is the goal the country's
tourist industry is striving to achieve. According
to an estimate by the WTO, in the year 2020 China
is expected to have 167 million tourist arrivals
from overseas, exceeding the United States,
France, Spain and Italy to become the biggest
tourist destination country in the world. This
shows international tourist circles' firm belief in
the inexhaustible appeal of China tours and the
strong vitality of China's tourist industry.

FOREIGN OFFICES OF CHINA NATIONAL TOURISM ADMINISTRATION

China National Tourist Office, New York
350 Fifth Avenue, Suite 6413, Empire State Building
New York, NY 10118, U.S.A.
Phone: 1-212-7609700
Fax: 1-212-7608809

China National Tourist Office, Los Angeles
333 West Broadway, Suite 201, Glendale, CA 91204, U.S.A.
Phone: 1-818-5457507, 5450666
Fax: 1-818-5457506

China National Tourist Office, London
4 Glentworth St. London NW1 5PG, U.K.
Phone: 44-171-9359787
Fax: 44-171-4875842

Office du Tourisme de Chine, Pairs
15, rue de Berri 75008, Paris, France
Phone: 33-1-56591010
Fax: 33-1-53753288

Fremdenverkehrsamt der VR China in Frankfurt
Ilkenhans Strasse 6
D - 60433 Frankfurt am Main, Deutschland
Phone: 49-69-520135
Fax: 49-69-528490

China National Tourist Office, Madrid
Gran Via 88, Grupo 2, Planta 16, 28013 Madrid, Espana
Phone: 34-1-5480011
Fax: 34-1-5480597

China National Tourist Office, Sydney
19th Floor 44 Market Street, Sydney NSW 2000, Australia
Phone: 61-2-92994057
Fax: 61-2-92091958

China National Tourist Office, Singapore
1 Shenton Way, #17 - 05 Rolina House, Singapore 068803
Phone: 65-2218681/82, 2219268
Fax: 65-2219267

China National Tourism Administration Tokyo Office
Air China Building, 2-5-2 Toranomon, Minato-Ku,
Tokyo, Japan 105
Phone: 81-3-35918686
Fax: 81-3-35916886

China National Tourism Administration Osaka Office
4f OCAT Building, 1-4-1 Minatochi, Naniwa-Ku,
Osaka, Japan 556
Phone: 81-6-6353280
Fax: 81-6-6353281

China International Travel Service, Hong Kong
6th Floor, Tower 2, South Seas Center
75 Mody Road, Tsim Sha Tsui, Kowloon, Hong Kong
Phone: 852-27325888
Fax: 852-27217154 (Office)
        852-27215931 (Japan Division)
        852-23118165 (Flight Division)

APPENDIX

CHRONOLOGY OF RECOGNITION OF WORLD HERITAGE SITES IN CHINA BY WORLD HERITAGE COMMISSION OF UNESCO

NAME OF HERITAGES	YEAR OF RECOGNITION
The Great Wall (Cultural Heritage)	December,1987
Peking Man Site (Cultural Heritage)	December,1987
The Imperial Palace of the Ming and Qing Dynasties (Cultural Heritage)	December,1987
The Mogao Caves (Cultural Heritage)	December,1987
Mausoleum of the First Emperor of Qin and Terra-Cotta Warriors (Cultural Heritage)	December,1987
Mount Taishan Scenic Area (Both a Cultural and a Natural Heritage)	December,1987
Mount Huangshan Scenic Area (Both a Cultural and a Natural Heritage)	December,1990
Jiuzhaigou Scenic Area (Natural Heritage)	December,1992
Wulingyuan Scenic Area (Natural Heritage)	December,1992
Huanglong Scenic Area (Natural Heritage)	December,1992
Ancient Building Complex in the Wudang Mountains (Cultural Heritage)	December,1994
The Potala Palace (Cultural Heritage)	December,1994
Confucius Temple, Residence and Confucian Family Cemetery (Cultural Heritage)	December,1994
Chengde Mountain Resort and Outlying Temples (Cultural Heritage)	December,1994
Mount Lushan Scenic Area (Cultural Landscape Heritage)	December,1996
Mount E'mei and Leshan Giant Buddha (Both a Cultural and a Natural Heritage)	December,1996
The Ancient City of Pingyao (Cultural Heritage)	December,1997
The Classical Gardens in Suzhou(Cultural Heritage)	December,1997
The Old Town of Lijiang (Cultural Heritage)	December,1997